CHILDREN

BY

CHOICE?

CHILDREN BY CHOICE?

Double standards,
population
and the planet

THE ISSUES
THE ENEMY
THE BATTLES
THE SOLUTIONS

BARBARA ROGERS

Author of *The Domestication of Women*

The information and commentary in this book are freely available for use provided that attribution is given to *Children by Choice* and to the author. Please contact the author via the website: **www.childrenbychoice.net**.

This book is an updated and revised version of the previously published book *A Matter of Life and Death: Women and the New Eugenics,* by Barbara Rogers (Brown Dog Books, 2018)

ISBN: 979-8-71667-267-3

ASIN e-book: BO8Z8CL78Y

Cover design by: Art Painter
Library of Congress Control Number: 2018675309
Printed in the United States of America

CONTENTS

PART THREE: BATTLES

PART FOUR: SOLUTIONS

INTRODUCING THE DOUBLE STANDARD

Children by choice: this is one of the greatest luxuries of modern life for almost all of us in countries where safe and effective family planning is freely available. Children by force is the grim reality for so many in the rest of the world, where the barriers to such services are impossible to get through. It is perhaps the biggest double standard in the whole rich world/ poor world divide. It is also the reason why the human population is growing beyond what our world can sustain, outpacing economic and social development, or the protection of the environment on which we all depend.

This has perhaps not been given priority for national and international action because the issue is around women. This is the biological reality: women hold the key to decisions about pregnancy and childbirth. While men (given the opportunity) can have dozens or even hundreds of children, women can have only those that their own bodies can carry and deliver into the world. Because of this simple fact, estimates of population are invariably done in terms of numbers of births per woman.

Without women, the world cannot have the next generation and it cannot have any future. It is women who bear all the physical and emotional costs of pregnancy, the toll on their bodies, the pain of childbirth, and most of the care and nurturing of babies and children. It is women who are aware of what it all means because they experience it directly. They do not need "experts" to tell them about it. Men do not have this experience, and surveys show that men generally want more children than women do. It makes sense: they have the pleasures or perhaps the status of having many children, but bear few or none of the personal costs.

There is a secondary reason why this is about women, and our choices: the current state of contraceptive methods. Most of these, with the obvious exception of condoms, are for women to use. It is easier to disrupt women's delicate endocrine balance and timing, which produces one egg a month, than to do the same for men and their production of millions of sperm. For many decades researchers have tried to produce a male contraceptive, one that maintains their sexual drive but makes their sperm infertile. At the same time it would have to have few or no side effects. Then there is the big question of whether women can trust some men to tell the truth about whether they are using any form of contraception which is not obvious. So it is back to women again.

The latest world population projections show this quite clearly. According to the United Nations, with the total human population at around 7.8 billion people, and growing at 80 million a year, the number of births to each woman would make all the difference between even higher levels of growth and stabilising our numbers. If half the women in the world had one less child it would stop population growth by the end of this century, reducing projections by three billion, and there could even be a small reduction in our current numbers (which many observers think is already too many). Although this book is not about the numbers - it is about individual decision-making - that is a sobering figure.

Family planning has always been part of women's culture, often with the knowledge held secretly from the men. Yet many of the traditional methods (with the exception of physical separation) are less secure, and less safe, than modern methods which have been developed over many years of trials, monitoring of patients, and continuous improvement. So the debate is largely about these safe and effective methods of today and whether they should be equally available to all. It is estimated that 200 million women worldwide have an unmet need for family planning: they do not want another child, or at least not yet, but lack the means to prevent it.

Taboos

For too many of the influential policy makers in international development circles, or even in the environmental movement and among women's organisations, the subject of children by choice is taboo. That does not stop better-off women, with access to health services in the wealthier countries, from taking full advantage of family planning for themselves, and so a double standard prevails. We would erupt in rage if there was any attempt to stop us using these services, yet many oppose it or remain indifferent about offering it for others: we have it, but you should not.

It is often claimed that some mysterious "traditional culture" in all non-western countries would make it impossible. How strange that many of us who benefit from good family planning are quick to deny it to others without asking what they really think. Some would call this patronising, even imperialist.

It would be hard to overstate the difficulty of debating family planning and "population" issues at the present time. There is so much known and written about the numbers, and yet the question of how women can make their lives better and safer through greater control of their own fertility is largely hidden, apart from the specialist organisations which keep a very low profile and tend to talk only to each other. The taboo is reinforced by those I am calling the Adamants: those men, and some women, who insist on all women having to bear "their" children. It is found most obviously in the anti-abortion movements, but there is also a strong undercurrent of opposition to contraception as well. Anti-abortion or "pro-life" movements are too often a cover for pro-natalism, especially in religious circles. The best way to reduce the number of abortions is to provide good contraception, and yet many "pro-lifers" are also against contraception. The message is: we will make you more children. You do not have a choice.

But consider this: a fictionalised version of this issue, Margaret Atwood's *The Handmaid's Tale*, has gone worldwide. She has often said there is nothing in her book that has not happened somewhere in the world, often repeatedly: women forced into sex, denied control of their own bodies, threatened if they try to resist, and forced to bear as many children as their bodies can produce. This is what hundreds of millions of women around the world experience in real life. Yet the connections between *The Handmaid's Tale* and real life are often ignored.

This is not rocket science. Remove the barriers to safe and effective contraception, backed up by early and safe terminations of unwanted pregnancies, and women will make sure that they have fewer and healthier children. Family sizes will fall. Community numbers will stabilise. Population growth would no longer be an issue. This is a difficult issue only because there are powerful vested interests in getting more and more babies: interests of power, electoral success and military ambition. That is what this book is about.

Finding the right words

The term "family planning" is a general one which includes both contraception and abortion, as well as sexual health, combatting sexually transmitted infections, and reliable information about our own bodies. "Family planning" is the best term available, not because women facing pregnancy are necessarily living in families - many young women facing unwanted pregnancy are on their own, and terrified. But if they do have a child they are also creating a small family. Incidentally, "family planning" could also mean planning not to have any children, which is one of the choices available to people in developed countries (including myself) and an important contributor to a reduction in population growth in these countries..

Modern projects and programmes have shown that women everywhere do want to be able to decide whether to have children, how many, and when. If there are barriers then it is about unfamiliarity with what is possible, prohibitions or misunderstandings often promoted by the pro-natalists, powerful community and religious leaders, the dictates of male partners or of or older people in their own families demanding more grandchildren. Given the chance, women vote with their own bodies. It has been estimated that half of all pregnancies are unplanned. That does not necessarily mean unwelcome, of course - some will be what is called a "happy accident" - but many of these pregnancies are most definitely unwanted. The proof of this is the huge numbers of abortions that take place around the world.

Some of the resistance to discussing this issue in the women's movement, even though they do want to improve the choices available to poor women, is in the degree of energy which is being devoted to trying to ban any discussion of numbers, or even the use of the word "population". "So you're in favour of 'population control' aren't you? That would be eugenics then!" Alternatively, and strangely, "If you refer to population you are blaming black women." These claims are deliberate silencing strategies, and they are wrong.

We cannot possibly discuss these issues by banning words, or banning numbers for that matter. Let us have a new approach which acknowledges population growth as an important and relevant issue, but sees the solution not in numbers but in individual choices. If we can maximise the funds available for family planning because of concern about population growth, its effect on the environment, and on economic development, then that is a necessary part of the case for enabling all women to have children by choice.

At the same time, an exclusive focus on "population" as in a "population bomb" and a panic about the numbers, creates real problems. The issue is not really about numbers, and certainly not about particular words. We cannot censor the word "population" but at the same time we need to see it as an abstraction, an unhelpful distraction from understanding the lives of the real people at the heart of this.

Many volumes have been written about "population" and the effect of increasing numbers of people on natural resources, the environment and climate change. Many of these studies, almost all of them written by men, end with the briefest possible reference to family planning. Even at their most generous the argument is: let's not examine this in too much detail but perhaps it might be a good idea after all… Alternatively, there may be a reference to tackling the problem by getting more girls into school. This may be an excellent objective in itself but it is at best a very indirect way to tackle the barriers to choice, and cannot have much impact as long as those barriers exist. Women with little or no school education also need the services.

We will never solve the problem by staying mesmerised by the numbers. We can deal with it only by focussing on individual needs and decisions, individual health and welfare, and the forces that are depriving people of their ability to make their own decisions. This book looks at some of the issues, and particularly the organised opposition to family planning and the promotion of pregnancy and birth at all costs. Our opponents are insisting that there should be more and more children, regardless of the suffering involved or the costs to society.

It has become a cliché that the personal is political, but it is certainly true here. "Population" is also personal as well as political. We need to decide which side of the debate to start from: global numbers of people, or individual needs? I will argue that it is the individual, and her choices, that are the key.

A matter of life and death

The barriers to family planning are closely related to the degree of poverty in which people live. It is no exaggeration to say that, especially for the poorest of the poor, this is about life and death. It is about births, synonymous with producing a new life - often in dangerous and difficult circumstances. The most basic decision we can make about life is whether to have children, and if so when and in what circumstances. It is also about death because of the huge numbers of deaths and injuries to women and their babies from a combination of poverty, inadequate maternity care, dangerous abortions, and poor health and nutrition. We are sometimes told that contraceptives are dangerous for a woman who is malnourished, yet that ignores the much bigger risk to her health from pregnancy.

If there is to be genuine development in poor countries, there should also be health. The Covid-19 pandemic has shown starkly that there can be no economic welfare without good (or at least good enough) health. Where people have access to universal basic health care, including family planning, adults are healthier and their babies also have a much better chance of good health and a good life.

At the moment many women and even young girls are being forced to have babies too close together, or when they are not physically or emotionally mature, and this carries a serious risk of death or permanent disability. It is closely linked to other issues which are much more prominent in the international agenda such as forced marriage, trafficking, preference for male children and neglect of females, female genital mutilation, legal rights, and exclusion from education and jobs.

Many babies are being born into a world where - if they survive - they will suffer from hunger, sickness or disability, with little or no education and poor prospects for the whole of their lives. They may have no job, no land and no means of earning a living. With increasing numbers of children, whole families may be plunged into deepening poverty.

For those who want to dismiss this as "population control", the reality of family planning is the exact opposite: access to our own birth control, and opposition to any attempts by others to control our decisions.

One doctor who decided to become a campaigner for family planning suddenly understood this issue when, after battling to save the life of a newborn baby, he was finally able to place the child in his mother's arms. The look of fear and even disgust on the mother's face, at the prospect of another mouth to feed when there was already too little to go around, shocked him into a realisation that not all babies have a real chance at life.

I was very struck too when reading of a dedicated Indian doctor who rescued children from slavery conditions in sweatshops and returned them to their families. One small boy, having been brought back to his home, was immediately told to leave again because there was nothing for him. "We don't want you." This is the reality of families with more children than they can possibly care for.

Overcoming the cruelties of nature

People, like all animals, have evolved to produce the next generation. Some animals have ways of controlling their own numbers, for example by feeding only the strongest chicks or by having smaller litters of pups when the area is becoming overcrowded. Humans do not have any such mechanism. It is up to us to use our personal and social skills to regulate our fertility so that we have healthy children and families.

Without effective contraception, which is so often the case in many parts of the world, there is a hidden epidemic of dangerous abortions as women try to terminate unwanted pregnancies. These often botched abortions lead to many health services being overwhelmed with casualties, while huge numbers of women die from abortions as well as child-birth. In many cases they leave their existing children as orphans, whose chances in life are the bleakest of all.

The world does indeed face a crisis of increasing human numbers, which have been building since prehistory and accelerating over the course of the last two centuries. Although birth rates are now actually declining, the survival of babies and infants is improving much faster. Obviously, better survival - thanks to improved health, nutrition and maternal and infant health care - is welcome. But until it can be matched with better choices about pregnancy, there is a serious imbalance which ultimately threatens the welfare of all. Rapidly growing human numbers are concentrated in the poorest areas of the poorest countries and this is an issue of extreme inequalities, within countries as well as between them. These areas often have the most fragile environments, which people have no choice but to exploit for survival.

Nature is cruel: human fertility, left unchecked, produces many more children than we can look after. Individual choice is key: our own ability to control the number and spacing of our pregnancies.

Part 1 of this study reviews why this is a critical issue, especially for women. For men it can be a matter of opinion whether there should be modern contraception, while for women it is truly a matter of life and death. I offer a brief overview of innovations in contraception and the innovative projects and programmes being offered now to introduce modern family planning. With the increasing sophistication in the delivery and evaluation of contraception and early terminations of pregnancy, these should be better publicised and made available across more regions and countries.

In Part 2 I then examine some of the issues and arguments, including the role of fundamentalism and the notion of eugenics - which I will argue has always been a pro-natalist and often racist ideology. I discuss the exaggerated fear of an "ageing society" as an argument for more babies, and the strangely modern evolution of the Catholic Church's crusade against family planning, now elevated almost above all other doctrines. They are not the only powerful body to be demanding more births - many Protestant fundamentalists are just as "pro-life" (or pro-natalist) as the Catholic church - but the Holy See/ Vatican is far ahead of other religious groups in its access to national and international decision-making and so requires special scrutiny.

In Part 3 I recall some of the arguments over this issue, and the advance of pro-natalists among the fundamentalists of all religions and sects, as well as among politicians and self-appointed "community leaders". I review the retreat of many western-based women's organisations in the face of the "Adamants", and the reluctance - until recently - of many environmentalists to challenge them. I also look at how the Vatican/ Holy See is leading the charge of conservatives against any international action which would improve women's access to safe and effective family planning.

Part 4 then puts forward a few ideas about how to present the issues, in the context of health needs and choices rather than sexual and reproductive "rights" which merely reinforce the opposition. I also suggest some of the initiatives that could be taken on the international scene to kick-start a new approach. These range from how to calculate national GDP to the connections with the environment and climate change, the integration of family planning into basic universal health services, alongside a new emphasis on health within the development process.

Some statistics are inevitable on this topic, but I have kept them to a minimum since the emphasis should be on individual and family needs, and a challenge to the silence which largely surrounds the issue on an international scale. We need to change the debate, break the silence, and trust the women as well as the men of the world to make their own choices, and decide how we can all move forward to a better life and a better world.

PART ONE

REMOVING

BARRIERS

Chapter one

MODERN CONTRACEPTION, SAME OLD DOUBLE STANDARDS

It is estimated that 121 million unintended pregnancies have occurred each year between 2015 and 2019, almost half of all pregnancies worldwide, most of them because safe and effective contraception was not available. Of these the majority (61%) were terminated. This translates to 73 million abortions. The estimates are produced by the Guttmacher Institute, which monitors the situation on a regular basis.

Well over 200 million women have an unmet need for family planning: 232 million women, according to the UN Fund for Population (UNFPA). This is where the problem lies. The issue of "population" is surrounded by the dry statistics of demography: abstract numbers and not individual people's lives. It is critical that we understand what unmet need really means: children born without the means to feed and care for them, an epidemic of abortions, the deaths of young women who should have their lives before them, and children left without mothers. Having more children than your health can sustain, or your family can feed and care for, is a tragedy. Dying during pregnancy or childbirth is a terrible reality for many millions of women all over the world. We rarely, if ever, have to confront this loss. But no discussion of "population" can be realistic unless we do.

"All I wanted was to get out of there"

I have chosen a few of the descriptions from Badakshan, Afghanistan by the photographer Alixandra Fazzina. This is inequality and poverty at its most extreme.

A widower sits with his orphaned daughter. Her mother died four years ago during childbirth after seven days in terrible pain, moaning and crying. He had prayed to keep her alive but there was no medical help to save her life. The little girl, who witnessed all of this, became withdrawn and cried all the time. She has now been sent away to live with her grandparents and will probably be married soon and have to face the same trauma herself. Her father has now taken another wife.

A heavily pregnant woman tried to make the two and a half hour journey on foot from her village to the nearest clinic, suffering from severe pain and bleeding. She never made it but had to give birth alone, hiding behind some rocks, then turned back with the newborn baby still attached to her and wrapped in a blood-soaked burka. Since then no woman in her village has dared to seek outside help while facing a difficult birth in case this happens to them.

A young woman lies on the operating table at a maternity hospital having arrived in great pain, with heavy bleeding and struggling to breathe, following a 12-hour journey by jeep across mountain roads. She is four months pregnant and has already had four miscarriages. Her husband has sold all their land to get her to the hospital. His first wife had died during childbirth.

A grandmother struggles to care for her orphaned granddaughter in one room. The child's mother was only 27 when she died in great pain during childbirth. "There was nothing I could do - I just had to stand by." They managed to find transport across the mountains for the seven-hour journey to the nearest hospital, but by the time they got there it was too late to save her life. The father has rejected the child, as is often the case when the mother dies in this way. The grandmother, although in deep shock, was the only person who would take her in. She and her granddaughter have no means of support and survive only through help from her neighbours, who are themselves struggling.

A 20-year-old woman, who is pregnant for the third time in three years, is afraid for her life when she finds it hard to breathe and has abdominal pains. She visits a female elder for help because she knows how many other women in her village have died during pregnancy or while giving birth. They are not allowed to leave the village to seek medical help and the traditional remedies are no use.

A traditional birth attendant is holding her empty tool kit in which she should have basic equipment to help with childbirth. Up to seven years ago she used flints for cutting and piles of earth for soaking up the blood. Now, following a training course seven years ago, she wants to use plastic gloves and sheeting, and sterilised razors and needles, but these are often unavailable.

> *"I always reassure the women in delivery, but there is nothing I can really do."*

From Nepal there is another report of too-frequent, unsupported and dangerous pregnancies as a threat to the lives of women. An account from the poor area of Accham by film maker Subina Shrestha, who was herself pregnant at the time, gives some sense of the fear that many women have:

> *"A nurse had tales of women dying while giving birth. She talked about women who begged to be saved but their family refused to take them to a hospital, and of women whose vaginas were hacked by village "healers" after their baby died inside them. No wonder our guide was so keen to have us around. It meant that we would not let her die."*

> *"Tales of women suffering in Accham could make any sane person's blood boil. Even if women survive one childbirth, they might die in the next one. If they have daughters, they are obliged to keep trying until they have several sons. Those who live through it all might have prolapsed uterus. When I think of the fate of a 13-year-old girl, it breaks my heart. Accham is like a black hole where women's dignity is destroyed. Even before the filming ended, all I wanted was to get out of there."*

"Trapped in poverty"

We can understand a little of what it is like for a few women in one community, but the sheer scale of this is almost beyond our imagination. Random and uncontrollable pregnancies are a huge threat not only to women's lives and health, but also the welfare of whole families and communities. Women's fear of pregnancy leads to about half being ended by abortion, most of these desperate and dangerous and leading to widespread deaths and severe injuries and disability. Globally, the numbers of these death far exceed most epidemics. In 2014, which saw high death rates from the Ebola epidemic, there were four times as many deaths from abortion.

There are an estimated 48 million abortions, 10 million miscarriages and one million babies born dead every year. It is estimated that 232 million women are unable to get family planning when they need it. The figures would be impossible to ignore if this was any other international issue. Planning for children, and the births and deaths that arise from women being unable to get modern contraception, are the biggest single issue for women worldwide. It is also very much an issue of poverty and inequality. The rate of deaths for women in childbirth in the least developed countries is 436 per 100,000 births, compared with just 12 in developed countries. In other words, deaths are 36 times higher in the poorest areas than the richest ones.

Unintended pregnancy is closely linked with the women's issues that are now on the international agenda. They include forced marriage, rape, female genital mutilation (FGM), sexual harassment and domestic violence, together with discrimination in education and jobs, and exclusion from the modern economy. It is particularly acute for the girls who are married off as children, sometimes even before puberty: we are talking here of child sexual abuse or rape, being forced to work without pay for the husband and his family, and being made pregnant before their immature bodies are ready and when childbirth is particularly dangerous, both for the girls themselves and for the babies. These are often treated as single issues but for the woman concerned it is all one: her whole life. Sex and pregnancy at too young an age, and births which are too closely spaced, impose a serious burden on women's health, and that of the babies.

Most of the women with an unmet need for contraception live in 69 of the poorest countries on earth. For many, there is no family planning service of any kind. There may be no health services at all, or at best a clinic run by a Catholic or Islamist organisation which excludes contraception and terminations altogether. UNFPA reports:

> *"the unmet need for family planning in developing countries is generally greatest among women in the poorest 20% of households."*

This particularly applies if they are less educated and living in rural areas, and is even more extreme for adolescent girls. They may be forced into sex with older men and have little power in the relationship, in some cases being repeatedly raped by their husband or partners. The UNFPA add that inequality in family planning access intensifies the divisions in society. Closing the gulf between women in income and employment will largely depend on enabling all women and girls to meet their reproductive needs.

> *"Inequalities in sexual and reproductive health and rights have implications that run from individuals to entire nations… A poor, uneducated woman in a rural area who cannot make choices about pregnancy will be unlikely to get an education or join the paid labour force. As a result, she will probably remain trapped in poverty and marginalization."*

The level of unmet needs closely mirrors levels of poverty. Just 2% of women in France have an unmet need, while in Samoa it is 46%. Overall, the levels of unmet need are twice as high among women in higher-income countries as in medium- and low-income ones.

Africa south of the Sahara is a particular area of need, together with Southern Asia, especially India, Indonesia, Pakistan and the Philippines. Almost half of the 44 countries with the required data have unmet need levels of over 20% of all women of reproductive age who are married or in a sexual union. For over a quarter of these countries this is over 30%. Even where some modern contraception is available (especially with condom-only programmes to combat HIV/AIDS) women and girls may not have the men's agreement to use it. A limited range of choices in many areas means that women and couples may not be able to get the most effective method for them.

"Almost three million babies die"

Within countries the inequalities are even more extreme. The greatest need is found among the poorest and least educated people, young unmarried women, and those in rural areas. This is also a feature of conflict zones and among refugees and migrants. South Sudan, for example, has one of the highest rates of maternal mortality in the world, together with one of the highest fertility rates of almost five children on average for each woman.

Maternal mortality also closely matches the levels of poverty. For mothers as well as for their infants, the risk of dying during or shortly after birth is 20-50% higher for the poorest fifth of households than for the richest fifth. In Chad, for example, only 1% of the poorest women are attended by skilled health personnel during delivery compared with 48% of the wealthiest women in that country.

A woman's lifetime risk of maternal death - the probability that a 15-year-old woman will eventually die from a maternal cause - is 1 in 160 in developing countries, compared to 1 in 3,700 in developed countries. The combination of poor general health and nutrition, pregnancies too young or too closely spaced, the lack of skilled health personnel to help with the birth, and dangerous abortions are all factors. For girls under 15 years old; complications of pregnancy and childbirth are the leading cause of death.

High levels of child marriage in some countries is contributing to this mortality, and so is the abuse and trafficking of girls. They simply do not have the information or the means to start protecting themselves, since there is very little information or guidance about sex and relationships for young people. At the same time, worldwide distribution of pornography portrays girls and women as sexual objects, the targets of sexual use by men, and rarely even mentions their need to consent, or for protection against unwanted pregnancy.

In 2017, the World Health Organisation estimates, an average of 810 women died every day from preventable causes related to pregnancy and childbirth, equivalent to one woman every two minutes, with a total of just under one million every year. About 300 million of their babies also die during or shortly after birth. And for every woman who dies, 20 or 30 encounter health complications which could have been prevented by modern medical techniques, with serious or long-lasting consequences. One of the most common is fistula, caused by the baby being in the wrong position or too large for birth, which leads to obstructed labour. Adolescent girls are especially vulnerable to this.

A good health service would proceed to a caesarean section to enable a safe birth in this situation. Without that, the woman is forced to go through days of exhaustion and agonizing pain.. Eventually the foetus suffocates. The un-relenting pressure on the soft tissue of the mother's womb greatly reduces the flow of blood to the soft tissues surrounding the vagina, bladder and rectum. The injured soft tissue can die and creates a hole (fistula) through to the bladder or rectum which will cause her to become incontinent, leaking urine or faeces through her vagina for the rest of her life. Not only is this horrible for the woman if it is left untreated but it can lead to her being shunned, thrown out of her family and excluded from her community.

For each woman who dies or is incapacitated, there is usually a family - often with several children - who are plunged into disruption, hunger and intense poverty. The risk to health is illustrated by the numbers of women who becoming pregnant again too soon after giving birth, endangering their own health and that of their babies. While more than 92% of mothers do not want to get pregnant again soon after childbirth, 61% of postpartum women in low- and middle-income countries are not using family planning methods. At least half of these women give birth again within an interval that is seen as unsafe. Even when a mother is using whatever contraceptives she can get, they may not be the safest or most effective methods.

If all unplanned pregnancies could be avoided, this would provide a huge boost to women's health and survival rates. It would also permit a much higher proportion of babies being born healthy, with a better chance of good nutrition and being able to move out of poverty.

The World Health Organisation reports:

> *"Maternal health and newborn health are closely linked. Almost three million newborn babies die every year."*

It's the contraception, stupid

Good sexual and reproductive health, as defined by the UN Fund for Population, is a state of complete physical, mental and social well-being in all matters relating to the reproductive system. It means that people are able to have a satisfying and safe sex life, the capability to reproduce, and the freedom to decide whether, when, and how often to have a child. To maintain one's sexual and reproductive health, women and men need access to accurate information and the safe, effective, affordable and acceptable contraception method of their choice. They must be informed and empowered to protect themselves from sexually transmitted infections. And when they decide to have children, women must have access to services that can help them have a fit pregnancy, safe delivery and a healthy baby. This is the ideal, and it is largely achievable by most people in the richer countries.

Improving maternal health was one of the eight Millennium Development Goals (MDGs) adopted by the international community in 2000. Under MDG5, countries committed themselves to reducing maternal mortality by 75%

between 1990 and 2015. This target has not been met: the reduction in that time, although a great achievement, is a long way short of the target at just 43%. Clearly, the failure to provide safe and effective contraception, alongside poor health systems and inadequate obstetric services, has been a major factor in this failure.

The new Sustainable Development Goals (SDGs) have a further target of reducing worldwide maternal deaths from 239 per 100,000 to under 70, with no country having more than double that. Comparing this with the rate in more developed countries of just 12, this should be the very least that can be expected. Unfortunately the target is seen as very difficult to achieve as long as there is so little funding for programmes to improve family planning services within a basic health structure.

Many commentators on the subject of population growth like to emphasise the role of girls' education, as if this was a panacea that will solve all the problems. This could be partly because they do not want to face the obvious: it's the contraception, stupid. And suggesting that women without formal education are incapable of understanding the issues around fertility and childbearing is patronising and offensive. It has also been proved wrong again and again by well-designed information and outreach programmes as I outline in the next chapter.

A recent survey of the evidence by Daphne Liu and Adrian Raftery does acknowledge the connection between a woman's formal education and the number of her children. Of the two factors, however, they conclude that family planning is more important. The effect of attending school on contraceptive choices is weak at the primary level, which is where most girls drop out of the system. It is seen mainly in young teenagers who manage to get to "lower secondary" levels. This effect is still much lower than is the case with family planning provision, as measured by contraceptive prevalence (the proportion using contraception). They conclude, in Raftery's summary, that while family planning is the critical element, the two factors can work together.

> *"Education gives women more opportunities as alternatives to having large families, while family planning gives them the means to achieve their goals."*

"Be fruitful and increase?"

The case for urgent action to remove the barriers to family planning world-wide should not be based on a "population" panic over birth rates. It rests on the need for equity, where poorer women can have the same choices as those in high-income areas and countries.

The world population of humans has indeed expanded rapidly, to the point where we now threaten the natural environment of the planet on which we live. Up to 1700 our population grew extremely slowly at only 0.04% a year. This was because high fertility coincided with almost equally high mortality among mothers and especially children. We can only imagine the devastation this caused. The order recorded from ancient times to the people of the book to "be fruitful and multiply" (better translated as "increase" since multiplication had not been invented at that time) was for a world where the numbers of premature deaths among women and children, as well as high levels of disease and death for everyone, threatened the very survival of small communities. Our world is the opposite, where it is our large numbers which threaten our future.

Our numbers have largely determined the course of world history. Once health improved and mortality started to fall, things changed rapidly - especially over the course of the 20th century. The much larger numbers of surviving children in western countries during the 19th and early 20th centuries had world-wide consequences with the mass migration of their people to colonise other countries and continents, often displacing the local people and leading to intensive conflict. After the second world war there was a "baby boom" where returning soldiers and their wives or partners were hurrying to start families, to compensate for long separations and the losses of family members from the war.

During the last two centuries human population numbers have risen seven times over. Over the last 100 years this accelerated, with global population growing by more than four times and as Max Roser puts it,

> *"You have just lived through the steepest increase of that curve. This also means that your existence is a tiny part of the reason why that curve is so steep."*

The fact that our own individual existence is a part of this suggests a powerful reason why it is so difficult to confront the issue. We need to remind ourselves that this is not about us, it is about how many babies will be born in the future, and how their own lives will be.

The rate of growth is now slowing all around the world, having reached peak population growth in 1968 with an annual rate of 2.1%. This has now fallen to just over 1% a year. But that is still 82 million extra humans, in a world which is still reeling from the rapid increases since the Second World

War. The totals also conceal the immense differences, where richer countries with good family planning generally have very low growth or in a few cases a decline, while increases in many poorer countries with few or no services are still increasing rapidly. Roser describes this as "an extraordinary moment in global history." He points out that in higher-income countries large families were a brief phenomenon of the 19th and early 20th century, which led to the sudden increase in our numbers. Before that, an average of only two children per family used to reach adulthood and many of these families actually lost all their children to early deaths.

> *"The future will resemble our past, except that children are not dying, but are never born in the first place."*

That depends, of course, on how well we remove the barriers to family planning for all, rich and poor, demolishing the double standard as we go.

People not population

Without reproductive health, especially modern contraception, efforts to promote health and wellbeing will not work. In particular the health of women and children, and their whole families, are likely to deteriorate.

According to the latest estimates by the respected Guttmacher Institute, current levels of contraception are preventing the deaths of 100,000 women and 1.8 million newborn babies every year. They are avoiding 144 million abortions, including 38 million illegal and dangerous ones, and 25 million miscarriages. Fulfilling the unmet need for modern contraception in developing countries would, each year, save the lives of another 70,000 women and half a million babies, and avoid 24 million abortions and 6 million miscarriages. If we were talking about an epidemic of disease on this scale, there would be an international scandal and huge mobilisation of resources to combat it.

It has been estimated that achieving universal access to sexual and reproductive health services by 2030, and eliminating unmet need for modern contraception by 2040, would deliver $120 of social and economic benefits for every $1 invested. Yet since the mid-to-late 1990s, donor assistance dedicated specifically to family planning has decreased dramatically in absolute terms. There has been some increase in donor support more recently, but not enough even to make up this shortfall. There is a huge need for more money. According to the Guttmacher Institute, fulfilling unmet need for modern contraception in developing countries would require an estimated doubling of current global investments from the current US$ 4.1 billion to US$9.4 billion annually.

One of the most constructive approaches to the issue of reproductive choice is as a health issue, with a focus of concern for the individual woman, her partner and their children. Although we have to be aware of the numbers, this is not a numbers game. Trying to tackle the issue in this way (books with titles like "Population Bomb", "Population 10 Billion", "Full House," or "Peoplequake") can play into the hands of those who want to portray us as wanting "population control" by outsiders, rather than our real objective of wanting control to be in the hands of the people concerned. A focus on numbers also caters to the obsessions of sectarians who want to increase their own group's population at the expense of others - a key element in so many conflicts. This is the subject of Part Two of this book.

At the time of writing there is a crisis in the funding of family planning programmes, and particularly the continuing supply of commodities. Christian Saunders of the UN Population Fund estimates that for every $1 million shortfall in contraceptive commodity provision, there will be 360,000 unintended pregnancies of which 150,000 will lead to induced abortions. There would be 800 additional deaths of the mothers, 11,000 deaths of the infants and an extra 14,000 deaths of children under five years old. These are sobering figures. Funding cuts by major donors like the US and UK are making things worse. For the women and children involved, the reality can be catastrophic.

No place for pessimism

It is often argued that attempts to provide contraception are resisted by poor people, who are slow to accept what is offered. Nothing could be further from the truth: where real choice is provided there is strong demand. The range of effective choices in contraception has greatly improved in recent years, delivery channels have become better, and contraceptives are safer and more effective than ever (although further research and development are still needed). Several developing countries have had very successful government programmes providing opportunities for real choice, which has resulted in much reduced maternal and child mortality and a reduction in numbers of births to replacement level, similar to many developed countries. Some of these have received support and encouragement from an international campaign to improve access, FP2020 (now FP2030).

The list of those making this commitment is not what you might expect. They include low-income countries like Bangladesh, Bhutan, Lesotho, Ethiopia and Rwanda as well as medium-income countries like Cambodia, Iran and Thailand.

Worldwide, although there is much still to be done there has been great progress over the last few decades. Compared to 1970, when only 36% of married or cohabiting women between 15 and 49 were using any kind of contraception - modern or traditional - that figure rose to 64% in 2015. Africa has moved from 8.2% to a still too low 33.4%. Many of these were not using the safest or most effective methods, and this needs to be addressed, but the change is remarkable. But it still leaves other countries lagging behind.

One thing that would accelerate the rate of change would be a full understanding of the economic benefits of modern contraceptive delivery. Not enough work has been done so far to quantify the return on investment here. However there are already some findings of greatly improved health and welfare, together with better household incomes. A study by the Population Reference Bureau in Bangladesh in 2009 found that long-term integration of family planning and child health services in certain areas produced better health and well-being than those in a similar comparison area. A typical woman of 38 in the service area had one less child, while her body mass index rose above the level of risk from undernutrition and her daughters also had a healthier BMI. The family was more likely to have their own source of clean water, the children were more likely to be vaccinated against crippling diseases, and the family as a whole had more money.

Another very useful review has been carried out by the service agency Marie Stopes International, which has outreach programmes in some of the poorest regions in the world. They estimate, based on their own experience and using publicly available data, that in a typical poor and fragile country around a third of the women want to limit pregnancies but are unable to do so. If just 5% of these women are given access to modern contraception, the effect on national welfare is substantial. GDP per capita for the whole population would increase by US$1,700. Completion rates for girls in primary school would rise from 69.9% to 73.3%. There would be an increase in the Gender Equity Index for that country of 2.5 percentage points. Reliance on foreign aid would fall from 32% to 29%, and there would be a decline in its ranking on the Fragile State Index from 91 to 87, moving it out of the "Alert" category. Clearly, if the investment were more substantial than that, the effects would be even more positive. We need more such analysis to make the financial case for contraception and safe abortion. Many decision-makers may be indifferent to the case in terms of women's and families' welfare, but money talks.

Another set of calculations has been offered by the World Bank with its Global Financing Initiative for health, which aims to introduce cost-effective integrated health care, especially for women and children. They estimate that it would cost just $25 per woman per year to provide integrated health care to women and newborn babies, including family planning, prevention of young teenage pregnancies, ante-natal and obstetric care, prevention and treatment for HIV and sexually transmitted infections, and nutrition support and care for the babies. The benefits would be "almost incalculable". These would include prevention of 52 million unintended pregnancies, 14.9 million dangerous abortions, 194,000 deaths of women, 2.2 million deaths of babies, and 121,000 HIV infections among newborns. They also calculate that poverty, with the stunting of foetal and children's growth, leads to a 26% reduction in their income as adults. This is a serious brake also on national GDP per capita, they add, where stunting alone is estimated to reduce national GDP by an average of 6%, rising to 8% in South Asia and sub-Saharan Africa.

References

Unpublished reports from Alixandra Fazzina from the website of Noor Images.

Subina Shrestha, "Birth in Nepal," *Aljazeera Witness*, 13 July 2012.

Daphne H Liu, Adrian E Raftery. "How Do Education and Family Planning Accelerate Fertility Decline?", *Population and Development Review*, 2020.

United Nations Department of Economic and Social Affairs, Population Division (2020). *World Family Planning 2020 Highlights: Accelerating action to ensure universal access to family planning* (ST/ESA/SER.A/450).

UNFPA, *The State of World Population 2019*. All other figures are from Unicef, WHO, the Guttmacher Institute and UNFPA.

"Underuse of modern methods of contraception: underlying causes and consequent undesired pregnancies in 35 low- and middle-income countries," *Human Reproduction* (2015) 30 (4), Oxford University, UK.

Max Roser, "Future Population Growth" 2019. Published online at OurWorldInData.org. Retrieved from https://ourworldindata.org/future-population-growth (Online resource)

United Nations, Department of Economic and Social Affairs,

Population Division, *World Contraceptive Use 2019.*

United Nations, Millennium Development Goals Gender chart, 2015.

WHO, Unicef, UNFPA, World Bank and United Nations reports.

Rachel Winnik Yavinsky and others, The Impact of Population, Health, and Environment Projects: A Synthesis of the Evidence, Working paper 2015, The Evidence Project, Population Council, Washington DC.

Newman, K. and Fisher, S. (2010) Population Dynamics and Climate Change: A PSN Briefing Paper. Population and Sustainability Network. Available at: http://populationandsustainability.org/wp-content/uploads/2014/10/Population-and-Climate-Change-Briefing-Sheet.pdf

Singh, S., Darroch, J.E.and Ashford, L.S. (2014) *Adding It Up: The Costs and Benefits of Investing in Sexual and Reproductive Health 2014.* New York: Guttmacher Institute and United Nations Population Fund.

Copenhagen Consensus Center (2014) *Benefits and Costs of the Population and Demography Targets for the Post-2015 Development Agenda.*

Population Reference Bureau paper 2009, "Family Planning and Economic Well-Being: New Evidence From Bangladesh," available from their website.

Marie Stopes International, "Time to Invest: The case for

contraception as an investment for the future," published on their website, 2016.

Christian Saunders, UN Population Fund, "Differential Pricing: UNFPA's Experience with Contraceptives," on the UNFPA website.

World Bank Group, *The Global Financing Facility: Country-Powered Investments for Every Woman, Every Child, 2016.*

Chapter two

WHAT WORKS: LOCAL KNOWLEDGE, INTERNATIONAL EXPERIENCE

It is sad how little is known about family planning in the wider development community about the success stories of family planning. Is this the best-kept secret on the international scene?

My case for a new approach would not be complete without some reference to the innovative development work that has been done around the world to improve contraceptive methods, break down the barriers to choice and extend services. I have selected a few examples to illustrate the wide variety of successful approaches.

First, we should quickly review what contraceptive methods are available. In the popular view there is only the hormonal birth control pill for women, or condoms for men, supplemented by sterilisation for women (by tubal ligation) or men (through vasectomy). Otherwise there is only the hit-and-miss rhythm method of abstaining from sex altogether during a woman's most fertile phase, which requires excellent trust and communication between the partners. Few of us could claim we have such a level of mutual support. But there is now a wide variety of methods which go way beyond this, backed by science and the rigorous testing of new contraceptives.

Perhaps the most significant are the LARCs (long-acting reversible contraceptives). They include injectables which deliver progestogen and last for several weeks each time. This previously required a trained health worker but in 2016 it was made much easier with the Sayana Press, a pre-filled, single-dose syringe and needle in an all-in-one package which can only be used once, so that no cross-infection can occur. It is very easy to administer or even to self-inject, as is done with insulin injections by diabetics. This important innovation is the result of three decades' work involving dozens of cross-sector partners, including pharmaceutical companies and a variety of governmental and private aid donors.

Other LARCs include implants under the skin, which can last for up to five years but can be removed at any time to restore the woman's fertility. There are also a variety of intra-uterine devices (IUDs) which are inserted into a woman's uterus. These are also long-acting and easily removed.

The US National Institutes of Health list a wide range of other types of contraception licensed for use there. They start with barrier methods: diaphragms, cervical caps, female as well as male condoms, and contraceptive sponges, which can all be used on their own or with spermicidal gels or creams. Hormonal methods include patches, vaginal rings, implantable rods, and pills which can be progestogen-only or combined with oestrogen. Intrauterine devices are available as copper or hormonal IUDs. A variety of shapes, sizes, formulas and makes are often available for each category.

In addition, emergency contraception after unprotected sex includes inserting an IUD or taking two hormonal "morning after" mifepristone and misoprostol tablets, up to five days after unprotected sex. Sterilisation now includes non-surgical implants for women which seal the fallopian tubes within around three months, as well as surgical tubal ligation for women or the much simpler vasectomy for men. Work has even been done on the rhythm method to make it more reliable, for example using phone apps to get the timing as precise as possible.

Forbidden fruit

The variety of methods available to meet different needs and preferences is astonishing, and the result of a huge research and development effort by public, private and voluntary organisations, with stringent controls from regulatory bodies to ensure safety as well as effectiveness. This is not to say that the list is perfect. Although the hormonal methods now use very small quantities compared with the early days of the contraceptive pill, many people would still prefer to avoid their use altogether and work is proceeding to develop a non-hormonal pill. There is also a need for a male contraceptive pill, which is quite difficult to achieve, and there is a new method now undergoing trials which uses a switch just under the skin of the scrotum to block or allow the flow of sperm into the ejaculate.

Although the range of possible methods is not perfect, in practice the contraceptive choices available are enough for most women and men to be able to avoid unwanted pregnancy safely and securely. In case of contraceptive failure, there is early termination of pregnancy either through medical abortion with the two tablets or a minor surgical abortion through vacuum aspiration, or dilatation and evacuation, as a day patient. In cases of foetal abnormality or a risk to the woman's life, a more serious surgical abortion may be used at a later stage. In most of the richer countries, these are available to those who want to avoid or terminate a pregnancy. In many poorer countries, they remain all too often a forbidden fruit and the only alternative is some kind of semi-poisonous medication or a crude amateur surgical procedure, often without sterilisation of the instruments or pain relief for the woman. In some countries all abortion has been made illegal, or allowed only in the most traumatic cases of rape or a threat to the woman's life. Such moves do not stop women seeking abortions, they merely make it much more dangerous to do so.

In some countries, although contraception is available it may be limited to a few methods which would not suit everyone. Worldwide, female sterilisation is the most common contraceptive method. This can be major surgery, with all the risks and complications that this implies - far more so than male vasectomy, which is far less common. While it may be the best option for many women, it has been used by some oppressive governments and authorities to sterilise women against their will. Its prevalence can also be seen as an indicator of the limited range of contraceptives being available to many women, especially those who want to delay pregnancies rather than stop them altogether.

In 2019, 24% of those who are currently using contraception - that is 219 million women - relied on female sterilisation. Three other methods have more than 100 million users worldwide: male condoms (189 million), IUDs (159 million) and the contraceptive pill (151 million). Overall, 45% of contraceptive users rely on permanent or long-acting methods (female and male sterilisation, IUDs, injectables and implants), 46% on a short-acting method (such as male condoms, the pill and various barrier methods) and just under 9% on traditional methods (including withdrawal, and variations on the rhythm method).

Worldwide estimates are one thing but there is enormous variation in what is available in different parts of the world. The best practice is to have a range of different methods available for women to choose from, with advice as to which would be most suitable for them as individuals, and monitoring and follow-up of any side effects - together with help for women to come off contraception when they want to get pregnant. In high-income countries and areas this is the actual situation, often provided by public health authorities. But in poor areas this is far from the case, and there may also be entrenched patterns of supply with little choice, and inconsistent supplies, with the result that the use of different methods varies widely.

In Eastern and South-Eastern Asia, IUDs are the most common contraceptive method used (18.6% of women rely on this method), followed closely by male condom (17%). In Europe and Northern America, the pill and male condom are the most commonly used methods (18% and 15%, respectively), while in Latin America and the Caribbean it is female sterilisation and the pill (16% and 15% respectively). In Oceania, the dominant method is the pill (17 %) and in Central and Southern Asia it is female sterilisation (22%). In Northern Africa and Western Asia, the two most common methods are the pill (11%) and IUD (10%). Sub-Saharan Africa is the only region in which injectables are the dominant method, with a prevalence of 10% among all women of reproductive age. A major reason for this is that women can use injectables without their partners knowing about it.

"Confidence and care"

There is a very mixed picture, of course, within regions, and some programmes with some governments - even in low- and medium-income areas - making great advances. I have outlined review a few of the many hundreds of projects on different continents which are finding ways to bring modern methods to those who most need them, and then offer a few snapshots of innovative practice. Any attempt to sum up the work being done is probably inadequate, given the scale and scope of it, but these offer a flavour of family planning in developing countries today.

Marie Stopes International (MSI) works in Tanzania, among many other countries, and has 11 clinics throughout the country's urban and peri-urban areas, serving a range of clients on middle to low incomes. With support from the

Government of Tanzania, they are working to reduce the 7,900 deaths of women every year from pregnancy and childbirth, and the estimated one quarter of all women who have an unmet need for family planning.

In urban areas they use bajaji (a type of three-wheeled motorised rickshaw) to bring services at home to women who cannot get to the clinics. However many rural women in Tanzania are in even greater need, living in remote areas where clinics and hospitals are scarce, too expensive to reach, and often lacking appropriately trained staff and equipment. At these government-run facilities condoms and contraceptive pills might sometimes be available, but stocks frequently run out. Longer acting (LARC) methods may be unaffordable, or rarely offered because staff do not know how to fit IUDs or implants, and may not have supplies.

A typical MSI rural team, in Kahama, includes one physician, two nurses, a driver and a government nurse, and uses specially equipped 4x4 vehicles to reach remote areas and hold sessions in local buildings or a blow-up marquee. Radio broadcasts and text messages tell people what is happening, and great care is taken to work with religious and other local leaders who can reassure their people that this is acceptable. Once assembled, the people are offered entertainment as well as information, through drama, comedy and group discussions. Often they use anatomical models, or pull out different types of contraception from their blue Choice Kits and demonstrate how they are used. People are encouraged to touch and hold these devices while hearing about what they do.

There have been many prejudices and misunderstandings about contraception in the outreach areas with many believing it to be bad for their health, or could even make them permanently infertile. The team may not change such opinions through a single session, but by returning many times with consistent high-quality treatments that are obviously safe and effective, they can make contraception a real possibility for all. Women can also choose the method that will suit them best, with many going for the LARC methods. In cases where the men are opposed to contraception they often choose injections, a method which is especially useful if they want to keep their treatment confidential from husbands and other family members who might not agree.

This kind of outreach is clearly working well. There are 600,000 clients for the family planning services, and a reduced reliance on unreliable methods such as condoms as people switch to the more effective long-acting, reversible methods. This has prevented an estimated 920,000 unintended pregnancies and the death of 2,300 women. In addition, over 400 government health staff have been given training in modern family planning methods. However a programme such as this is expensive to deliver. Until there are serious increases in funding for family planning it will not be available to all who need it. In the target areas there will perhaps be less need for educational work as family planning and basic health care become more routine. Some resources can then be moved to new areas. This will take long-term and consistent funding and commitment, and the big question is whether international sources of aid will be able to sustain this.

In Guatemala the emphasis has been on working with traditional birth attendants, many of whom have inherited the role from other women in their own families, to support the Mayan women of Santiago de Atitlan. Many of these "comadronas" are older women who have worked for long periods in the region but received little training in modern methods. A small, twice-weekly Comadrona School of POWHER (Providing Outreach for Women's Health Education and Resources) has been set up where techniques can be learned but, just as important, the women can discuss their own experiences and how to combine old traditions with modern methods. A reporter from the US, herself medically qualified, was full of admiration for the women:

> *"I was immediately humbled by the real world experience and skills these comadronas possess. They think through medical cases in the classroom, but their work takes place in the wider community."*

She was invited to make home visits with them for ante-natal care.

> *"While I found myself hesitant with my hands… the comadronas beside me channelled the knowledge they had gained from belonging to a cultural tradition and especially the school. They went about their work with confidence and care."*

"Best friends"

In Afghanistan, a different approach has been taken with a course set up for young people to study midwifery, including family planning. They all come from Daikundi, a mountainous region dotted with isolated green valleys and one of the most remote and hard-to-reach areas of the country. All of them have been selected by their neighbours, communities and village leaders to take a written exam, and the most successful are brought to Kabul for the course. The students and their families sign a commitment that they will return to the village once they finish their studies. Many of the young women come from families where their own mothers and grandmothers died in childbirth. One girl described the death of a woman in her community:

> *"She lost a lot of blood and the placenta was retained. There was no midwife and she died. Her two children survived, but they died months later because the adopting families didn't have enough resources to take care of them."*

The project, managed by UNFPA in conjunction with the Afghan government and international aid donors, was set up after the people in local communities refused to accept mobile health teams and doctors. The new approach, according to Dr Molakhial of UNFPA, was intended to:

> *"actively involve the community in the process, guaranteeing their ownership from the very beginning."*

The project is a success because midwives return to their own communities with new skills, and also a new status. Each midwife runs a Family Health House that provides maternal, newborn and child care for between 1,500 and 4,000 people.

The midwives also do outreach work with the community and with family decision-makers, to reach other girls and young women in their communities who are not getting access to information or health care. They are supported by mobile health teams offering technical and managerial assistance to the new midwives once or twice a month, and also providing vaccinations and other primary health care. There are 82 Family Health Houses and nine mobile health teams in three provinces, with nine more coming into service.

Telecommunications are key to work in Nepal. This provides support and counselling on sexual health matters through a free helpline called Meri Saathi ("My Friend")" advising on a wide range of issues from safe abortion, contraception and safe sex to masturbation, penis size and menstruation. In mountainous Nepal, where it can take a woman days to get to the nearest primary healthcare centre, there is little accurate information apart from this. Sex before marriage is taboo, and so is discussion of sexual matters. The call centre is a lifeline for thousands of younger Nepalis. This is critical because, for example, abortion is legal during the first twelve weeks of pregnancy but many do not know this. Dangerous abortion is common and often self-inflicted with the insertion into women's bodies of iron bars and the like, accounting for more than 5% of recorded maternal deaths.

The telephone service has proved very popular, going from 150 calls per month to 150 every day, and is being expanded. Many of the calls are from adolescent boys asking about masturbation as well as sex in general, while young women are mainly concerned about unwanted sexual advances and harassment, contraception, menstrual pain and access to safe abortions. Some are desperate to keep their contraceptive use secret from their husbands, who may be older and interested mainly in having sons regardless of their wives' health and welfare. The success stories include a call centre operator persuading a mother not to force her 14-year-old daughter into marriage, and enabling thousands of women to avoid pregnancy when the time is not right for them to have a child.

These projects are just a few examples out of hundreds of health and family planning programmes around the world: a mixture of high-quality medical interventions which can offer the best choice of methods with medical backup if needed, and locally based advocates and midwives who come from the community, know how to communicate with the people, and have their confidence. Whether it is Ita Ouali ("best friends") in the war-torn Central African Republic, midwives in displaced people's camps in Myanmar, or Lady Health Workers in Pakistan, recruiting and training local women is often the key to a successful programme. This can be especially important in areas of conflict, high migration or refugee situations. The women and children involved are among the most vulnerable to abuse, exploitation and every kind of disadvantage.

"Difficult to talk about"

A number of initiatives have been developed by the UN Population Fund (UNFPA) for vulnerable young people, such as one in Mongolia. The "Y-Peer" scheme trains young volunteers to offer support to others who may be isolated, vulnerable and separated from their families in a rapidly changing society. They also offer information and access to health facilities, including contraception. One of the young teenagers they helped, who had been contemplating suicide, said

"Y-Peer saved my life. For that, I am so thankful."

In Nepal there is a programme in a remote region, Baitadi, where astrologers, shamans and priests have come together to persuade families not to force their children into premature marriage, sex and childbirth. When parents bring a girl's "cheena", an astrological chart, this is likely to mean preparations for her marriage. Astrologers say the parents often lie about their daughter's age, but the birth date on the cheena is always accurate. They can then advise the parents to delay the marriage until she reaches the legal marriage age of 20.

Also very important is relating to men in the community. Men typically want more children than women do, since they are not the ones experiencing pregnancy and birth, and most play a lesser role in feeding and nurturing the children. Their understanding of the issues, however, can be crucial and there are many family planning programmes which reach out to the men for their support and participation. One example of this is the Schools for Husbands in rural Niger, West Africa, where modern contraception is only just starting to be introduced in many areas and death rates for women are still extremely high. The country was ranked last on measures of gender equality in the 2013 Human Development Report, and men have been expected to take all the decisions in the household.

Starting in 2008, men have been invited to the local health centre to discuss issues of women's health and child-bearing. When the initiative was launched, few thought it would succeed.

"Years ago, it would have been difficult to talk about such issues with men in this village,"

said Almoustapha Boubacar, the manager of Maiki health centre. Not all men are invited: members must be married, at least 25, and accepting of women's participation in community life. These men become opinion-formers and role models within their communities, and some also work in collaboration with a group of women. They have provided some practical support to the health centres, doing building and decorating for example, and become effective in raising awareness in their communities about women's need for family planning and medical care for childbirth - although there are still some men who refuse to even discuss these issues. Meanwhile, the numbers of women coming to health centres has considerably increased in the areas where these schools for husbands are operating. Change can take a long time, but with help from a core of supportive men it is on the way.

Another innovative approach is the distribution of vouchers for women's health and contraceptive care. A scheme in Western Uganda sold vouchers at well below cost, redeemable against an approved list of high-quality services and medications for safe childbirth, treatment of infections, and family planning. A previous trial had shown that using vouchers simplified the targeting of sales to the poor, minimised administration, and controlled costs for the project overall. Voucher Community-Based Distributors (VCBDs) travelled around the villages to explain the benefits of using a clinic for delivery or to access other treatments. Using their local knowledge and the oral traditions of the villages they visited, VCBDs raised awareness of the scheme and generated lively community participation, with strong sales of the discounted vouchers. A problem arose when many of them left for a while to work for a political party in national elections. Overall, however, it was a great success.

The project set out to provide 50,456 safe deliveries and 35,000 treatments for sexually transmitted diseases (STDs). By December 2011, when the project closed, more than 136,000 people had been independently verified as having received a range of reproductive health services. Mobile phone technology made project communications and data management more efficient and the project successfully demonstrated that critical project transactions can be sped up, and errors reduced, by using text messaging. A 2010 user satisfaction survey conducted by the Population Council found that 94% of voucher users said they were satisfied with the quality of health care services, compared with 76% of patients who did not use vouchers. The project's success resulted in the Government of Uganda committing additional funds of US$3 million to support the development of new voucher projects.

Another innovative project with potential for wider use is in Indonesia, where there was a family planning service but with relatively low quality. Yayasan Cipta Cara Padua works to involve leaders and statutory authorities at local level to implement the government's Kampung KB programme to revitalize and improve the existing services, with a particular emphasis on improving the range of choice of contraceptive methods and the quality of delivery and medical back-up.

Health and environment

Alongside these large-scale health promotion schemes there are increasing numbers of smaller-scale Population, Health and Environment (PHE) projects, which use an integrated approach to preserve fragile environments and livelihoods. These use technical expertise and innovation for sustainable agriculture or fisheries through conservation of soil, water and wildlife; introducing alternative sources of income; and improving hygiene and public health. Alongside this there are health services, including family planning, to help people to reduce unintended pregnancies and so relieve the pressure of increasing human numbers on those areas - in other words, to make them more sustainable for present and future generations.

Alongside the projects motivated by health concerns, there are now increasing numbers which offer the same family planning services alongside environmental work to improve people's incomes without encroaching on natural ecosystems, water resources and wildlife.

One of the pioneers is Blue Ventures, in Madagascar. They are working on marine research and conservation:

> *"We work in places where the ocean is vital to local cultures and economies, and are committed to protecting marine biodiversity in ways that benefit coastal people."*

They started by surveying coral reefs, where the local people were worried about the decline in their catches, and agreed with them to close off a small section of their octopus fishing area for a few months. When this was reopened there was a huge increase in landings and therefore people's incomes. As news spread, neighbouring communities started copying this approach and combined to create a locally managed Marine Area. Temporary fishery closures have now "gone viral" along much of the coastline of Madagascar. Alongside this there is a community health programme, known locally as Safidy or "Freedom to Choose". Local women are trained to offer family planning and other health services, selling contraceptives at a small profit which they can keep for their own use. The health promoters are also offering basic health prevention measures such as mosquito nets, water purification equipment and oral rehydration salts for diarrhoea. The Blue Ventures outreach team regularly tours 32 coastal communities to discuss sexual and reproductive health, water purification and natural resource management. Smartphones are being introduced for communication and monitoring of the programme.

More recent initiatives have been taken by the Margaret Pyke Trust, based in London with 50 years' experience in reproductive health and training. They have projects in Uganda and South Africa working with conservation and other organisations. One has the aim of conserving the national bird of Uganda, the threatened Grey Crowned Crane, together with the wetlands where they nest in Rukiga District. They are undertaking habitat restoration and soil and water conservation, together with health and family planning services. The wetlands are crucial for providing water for the people, while removing the barriers to family planning, they argue, is crucial to people's lives and livelihoods as well as conservation of the wildlife.

Queuing round the block

Mass communication - this time in the form of soap operas - lie behind some of the most interesting initiatives in this field. Even where people have access to family planning, social attitudes and prejudices may mean that there is a lack of confidence in it: fear of side effects, religious opposition and couples' inability to talk to each other about sex and pregnancy. To get people thinking realistically about these issues, TV and radio drama series have proved very effective. The Population Media Centre produces locally written dramas in which key characters embrace such things as family planning, schooling for girls and other social and health issues. Researchers typically spend weeks talking to people in the target community, identifying the issues that matter most to them, before writing the script.

The idea of combining drama and public health was first developed in Mexico in the 1970s by Miguel Sabido, a television executive who believed that national welfare mattered as much as ratings. His shows promoting literacy and family planning became smash hits and generated impressive impacts. The year that Sabido's first programme, *Ven Conmigo*, appeared, the number of people signing up for government literacy classes jumped more than eight times. Following the run of a second show, *Acompaname*, sales of over-the-counter contraception spiked by 23%. Radio and television dramas inspired by Sabido's model have now appeared in dozens of countries.

> *"This is not a one-hour after-school special, or a one-minute public-service announcement,"*

says Arvind Singhal, a professor of communication at the University of Texas-El Paso who has researched the impact of such shows.

> *"These are programs that play themselves out over hundreds of episodes. If the programme is good, then you not only grab attention, but you grab it over a period of time."*

There is evidence of dramatic results in the 45 countries in which they have aired. For example, in northern Nigeria a radio serial was heard regularly by more than 70% of the population, and a study found that about two-thirds of those seeking contraception cited the programme as a motivating factor. Those who listened to it also reported wanting fewer children than before. In Ethiopia, during the two and a half years a similar radio series was broadcast, 40% of listeners reported using modern contraceptive methods compared with 25% of non-listeners. Communications of course have to be accompanied by good service provision, otherwise people can simply be frustrated when they try to make changes.

A further success has been reported from a multi-agency project using local radio in Burkina Faso, a very low-income country in the Sahel region of West Africa. The project, led by Development Media International, compared regions covered by the scheme with a control group of areas that were left outside. Results were then independently evaluated, and showed that using radio improved family planning outcomes on a large scale. This evaluation included focus group discussions with hundreds of participants to understand the barriers and enablers to the use of modern contraceptives and family planning generally.

The conclusion was that lack of access and fear of possible side effects such as infertility were common barriers to change, alongside a lack of decision-making power for women. Key messages were then developed for the scriptwriters who created motivational and informational radio spots, plus drama segments for phone-in shows.

Altogether there were 72,000 broadcasts on eight radio stations in six different languages, with ten brief radio spots per day every day for 30 months. The results were remarkable, doubling the use of modern contraceptives in local clinics. Modelling suggested that if there was a national radio campaign it would lead to an additional 225,000 women in the country using modern contraceptives, at a cost of just $7.70 each. A number of other African countries with low rates of contraceptive use are now signing up to similar multimedia campaigns. Unfortunately the whole scheme has been threatened by the sudden 85% cut in funding for family planning by the UK aid programme., although most of this will be covered by big charitable donors

Sometimes even adverse publicity can work. A few years ago when the injectable contraceptive Depo Provera was first made available, there was a campaign against it in some European countries, some of it inspired by pro-lifers. They exaggerated the supposedly terrible side effects and called for it to be banned, especially in developing countries. The attacks on Depo were repeatedly aired on radio and TV in Tanzania. Clinics there were amazed when women started walking long distances and queuing round the block for it. It seems the women got the message about preventing unwanted pregnancies and saw this as far outweighing any fears about side effects. Perhaps they were hearing the awful warnings about this new contraceptive in the way that the Kremlinologists of the Cold War used to read and listen to Soviet media: ignoring the propaganda while looking for clues to the real situation.

Any country can

Many of the programmes outlined above are successful because they have the backing of their national governments, even though most of the funds, expertise and personnel are brought in from outside. Increasingly, now, governments of many lower-income countries are starting to perceive the importance of modern contraception for their countries' future welfare and prosperity.

From the very poorest (Bangladesh, Bhutan, Ethiopia) to the strongly Muslim (Iran, Indonesia, Malaysia) or Catholic (Mexico, Cuba, Peru, Costa Rica) and with the worst history of ethnic conflict (Rwanda) to middle-income countries (South Korea, Thailand) many governments have shown that good family planning policies and programmes are possible. Among the most improved countries in this regard are two African states, Sierra Leone and Lesotho - both of which have emerged from a background of conflict and extreme poverty.

Where there is almost universal access to contraceptive services, the disadvantage suffered by the poorest women almost disappears and this is a serious contribution to increased equality among households. It is also a factor in economic growth. The Republic of Korea is an example of the "tiger economies" of Asia which have managed to turn their countries around.

> *"Investments in health, including reproductive health services, coupled with investments in education, contributed to an economic 'miracle', opening opportunities for all,"*

according to the latest review by the UNFPA. It is often forgotten that Japan, too, achieved its "economic miracle" after the disasters of the Second World War and a postwar "baby boom" by providing and promoting family planning and legalising abortion.

In Bangladesh, one of the poorest and most densely populated countries in the world, 61% of currently married women in a 2100 survey said that they were using some form of family planning, a level comparable to developed countries, and the total fertility rate has declined steadily to 2.3 children per woman.

One of the most striking success stories is that of a small Pacific island nation, the Maldives. We might think that being a small country, improving women's and children's health and survival rates and offering modern family planning would be simple. In fact it is very difficult because of the problems of serving many small and scattered islands. The 25-year campaign to improve women's reproductive health, with a family planning campaign and huge improvements in obstetric care, has resulted in a remarkable 90% drop in maternal death rates. The Health Ministry started with in-depth reviews of all maternal deaths, helping planners to understand the causes. Health workers then received additional training and were deployed within the islands and atolls to provide home visits.

Close monitoring proved essential, particularly for women with high-risk pregnancies. At the same time family planning information and access were improved. Community health workers made home visits to tell women about the benefits of planning their pregnancies. The government disseminated information via the mass media, using dramas and songs about all aspects of reproductive health from contraception to nutrition and safe childbirth. UNFPA increased the quantity and variety of contraceptive products available, including male and female condoms, oral contraceptives, intrauterine devices and implants. This is an outstanding example of local, national and international organisations working together over an extended period of time to turn around a disastrous situation for women and make this country one of the best for health in the developing world.

If they can do it, any country can.

No to coercion

There have in the past been so-called "family planning" programmes based not on choice but on coercion. These have demonstrated not only that they are wrong in principle, but are counter-productive by giving contraception a bad name in areas where incentives or penalties have been used. An obvious example is that of government programmes in India, which set up sterilisation camps and either offered people money to accept the operation or gave financial inducements to officials to persuade people in without explaining what it was. Medical back-up was clearly lacking, or very inadequate.

The result was an enormous amount of distress, among people who perhaps did not understand that this was a permanent end to their fertility but had little or no choice about it. Too many people suffered greatly from health complications. The programme sparked an angry resistance to the idea of all family planning in the areas concerned, and helped to make the notion of "population control" even more of a taboo subject internationally. What is less recognised is that the programme operated mainly in North India, while in the south of the country services were voluntary and were well accepted by people. This, combined with the greater autonomy of many women in the South, contributed to the wide gulf in fertility rates that prevails between North and South India now, and the social and economic benefits of smaller families now being felt in the South.

The other, and most important case of enforced contraception is of course China, the country with the biggest population in the world. Its "one child" policy for many

Chinese families was notorious for its cruelty. Women were forced to abort female foetuses, and newborn girls were often abandoned because the family insisted that if there was only one child it must be a boy. Sex selection has also led to a huge imbalance in the ratio of boys to girls, with all the social tensions caused by this. Unknown numbers of babies were born who became "non-persons", unable to become legal citizens and excluded from education and social support because their parents could not pay the fine or bribe for the "extra" child and therefore could not register the birth. Unmarried women and couples were fined if they had a baby, and their child was also excluded from registration to become "non-persons".

The Chinese "one child" policy was accompanied by rampant corruption as implementation of this government policy was left to the provinces. Many local officials demanded bribes for allowing children to be born and registered, favouring some families while penalising those who resisted. The policy, which always had exemptions for many ethnic minorities and rural areas, has now been modified to allow two children per couple. However, the official controls on people's choices about pregnancy and birth remain in place.

It has been argued that all this cruelty was completely unnecessary since birth rates were already declining rapidly in China before the "one child" policy was introduced, and if the same effort had been put into good health provision and family planning choices this could have resulted in a similar drop in family size, and therefore the national population. Lifting the limit to two children per family did not have the expected effect of greatly increasing birth rates since couples, especially in the cities, decided that they could not afford another child, or would find it difficult to care for two when both parents were working. These constraints are severe enough to lead to Chinese officials now worrying about a fall in population numbers. In 2021 the Chinese census showed a continuing increase, but a very small one at 0.53% a year. While the working population remained stable, the proportion of over-65s rose steeply and the proportion of children rose by less: 1.35% over the ten years.

All this would seem to point to a stabilising population, but Chinese officials decided that they now had to promote births. Premier Li Keqiang said they would "promote the realisation of moderate fertility" and "an appropriate birthrate" to increase the numbers of children, presumably to keep wages down and therefore competitiveness for their export industries against other developing nations. China's central bank has also called for an end to all birth limits, and to "encourage childbirth". The habit of imposing controls on people's choices about children has certainly not gone away in China.

The use of coercion to limit some births has not gone away either. It has emerged that the Uighur people in Xinjiang province are being subjected to extreme measures to reduce births, including forcible abortions and sterilisations. Arguments are ongoing as to whether this, together with other coercive policies, amounts to genocide. It is certainly a contravention of human rights standards by any definition.

The other example of government attempts to force people to limit the size of their families is Myanmar, which tried to impose "population control" on the Rohingya minority. This soon developed into a programme of forced evictions and the burning of villages, accompanied by horrific violence and the deliberate killing of large numbers of Rohingyas, including women and children, in a campaign which has itself been described as genocide.

Coercion has no place in family planning programmes: personal choice must be the key. The case of China and its notorious "one child" policy, in particular, has served to discredit the cause of family planning internationally, and especially in the rest of Asia. It is essential that they and others move as quickly as possible to provide health and family planning services that would enable the people, not the State, to make decisions about their own lives.

Must do better

Perhaps one of the most crucial indicators of progress in family planning is the willingness of so many organisations and governments to evaluate their services in order to keep improving them. In a landmark report from the FP2020 (family planning 2020) campaign run by UNFPA with money from the Gates Foundation, they reveal that some of the targets - 120 million additional users by 2020, with universal access to modern contraception by 2030 - are falling short at the half-way mark, and require some serious work on the bottlenecks if the final goals are to be achieved.

> *"The richness of the data now available enables us to peel back the layers and study the situation on a country-by-country basis. What emerges is a strikingly varied landscape of progress. A number of countries have registered immense gains in contraceptive use; other countries are moving more slowly; some countries appear stalled... This knowledge is part of the toolkit*

we take into the second half of the initiative. We also bring with us a deeper understanding of how family planning services reach, or fail to reach, specific sub-populations of women and girls. The evidence base is growing for a wide range of issues and interventions, including youth-oriented approaches, method mix diversity, stock-outs, contraceptive discontinuation, rights-based programming, and postpartum family planning. The resulting insights can help us shape more effective programs, investments, and policies to reach women and girls with the services they need."

They also point to three other main areas for future focus: accountability in terms of returns on money invested and assessment of outcomes; partnerships, making donors work more effectively with government and co-operating better with each other; and youth, meeting the urgent contraceptive needs of young people in new and more effective ways.

There is a dilemma here, and it is largely a financial one: we would all want the widest range of contraceptive choices, backed by state-of-the-art obstetric and gynaecological health facilities and medical backup. Enormous amounts of work have been done to make this possible, and much more affordable for individual users. And yet the money is not there to achieve this in all parts of the world at the same time and in fact the existing programmes face uncertainty about funding, and real cuts especially from the US and UK at different times.

A bad atmosphere around this issue is also created by is the constant scrutiny of services by opponents to discover any shortfall in care, real or often imaginary, that they can broadcast to the world as evidence for their claim that family planning is itself harmful and wrong. The truth is that no medical procedures are perfect and recognising this is crucial to improving the services. Meanwhile the opposition never mention the horrific record of deaths and injuries where there are no such services. The UNFPA points out that countries with low rates of family planning services for the poorest women also have the most inadequate ante-natal and maternity services, and the highest death rates for women and babies.

It is critically important that we continue working to ensure the highest levels of effectiveness and safety within the very limited budgets which are being allocated to this. At the same time these budgets need to be greatly increased if real choice is to be achieved everywhere it is needed.

Lives depend on it. The work goes on.

Resources

"What are the different types of contraception?" United States Department of Health and Human Development, National Institutes of Health website.

United Nations Department of Economic and Social Affairs, Population Division, *World Fertility and Family Planning 2020:*

United Nations Department of Economic and Social Affairs, Population Division (2019), *Contraceptive use by method 2019.*

For details of family planning programmes see the websites of UNFPA, Marie Stopes International, and FP2020 (Advance Family Planning) and other aid providers. Family Planning 2020 (FP2020), part-funded by the Gates Foundation, is also doing important research and outreach work.

"China's population growing at slowest rate in generations," *The Guardian,* London, 11 May 2021.

Bangladesh 2011, Demographic and Health Survey.

UNFPA, *The State of World Population 2017.*

FP2020, *Momentum at the Midpoint 2015-2016.*

PART TWO

KNOW

YOUR

ENEMY

Chapter three

RACISM, NATIONALISM, FUNDAMENTALISM, EUGENICS

How many times do we have to hear the accusation that enabling women to choose means "eugenics"? This is meant to be a word to strike terror in the heart of those who advocate any kind of free choice when it comes to having babies. It is sometimes claimed that our promotion of contraception is promoting a policy of selective human breeding controls which are somehow in conformity with the racial policies of Nazi Germany. The reality is the exact opposite of this: the real advocates of eugenics are the modern pro-natalists who promote maximum births in their own particular group by setting up barriers to family planning. Eugenics always means coercion, depriving individuals of any ability to make their own decisions about children. Voluntary, informed family planning - enabling control by women and their partners - is the opposite.

The early eugenic ideas of the late 19th and early 20th centuries meant changing the population by promoting births among some people (the educated middle and upper classes especially) while stopping or discouraging them among those living in poverty. There were certainly racist overtones to the debate, with some claiming that Europeans were somehow superior and therefore should have more children.

Others thought humanity could be "improved" by eugenics, selecting for intelligence and genetic health for example. The idea varied according to whether it was promoted by people of either the Right or the Left for very different reasons, ranging from helping individual women in need to controlling whole populations. They included such notables as the American black rights advocate WEB DuBois and the leading British economist John Maynard Keynes. Some advocates of family planning, notably Margaret Sanger in the US, used the language of eugenics to further the cause of individual choice through birth control. This may have been her defence against vicious attacks on early family planning advocates by right-wing eugenicists who opposed this choice on principle. Those people, as one Catholic bishop and eugenicist wrote to her, argued that "the races of northern Europe" were

> *"doomed to extinction, unless each family produces at least four children,"*

.

"Every child is a battle"

The Nazis picked up this extreme right-wing and racist version of eugenics and made it their own. They went much further than the previous advocates of course, killing millions of people they considered the wrong "race" while encouraging or even forcing women they called "Aryans" to bear the maximum number of children possible.

It is important to understand what the Nazis' eugenic policy really meant: this was at the heart of their theories and not some fringe idea, and it was played out in the lives and deaths of millions of people. Heimlich Himmler, using his elite SS troops, organised the systematic destruction of huge numbers of "other" babies and children, starting with disabled or supposedly "defective" children in Germany itself. Once extended across Europe their eugenic policies focused especially on Jewish and Roma people, including children, but also many of the Slavic "races" in eastern Europe. They murdered the children alongside their mothers and whole families inside the concentration camps and in the killing fields outside. Millions of people in the occupied countries were also starved, deported and put into forced labour, which resulted in yet more deaths.

It was this same Himmler who set up the *Lebensborn* (Fountain of Life) programme intended to produce racially and ideologically "pure" children for the Nazi cause. Half a million children from Germany and all over Europe who were judged "racially correct" were taken away from their families and placed in the SS Lebensborn institutions, where they were treated very harshly to indoctrinate them either as Nazi soldiers, or as mothers for the next generation.. The surviving children, now in their 60s and beyond, say they have felt "lost" for their whole lives.. Those taken to the institutions as toddlers talk of sitting on the windowsills endlessly looking out, hoping that their mother or father would come for them.

The racist attitude to babies and children was not confined to the elite but was deeply entrenched among many of the soldiers. A new book on German prisoners of war, drawing on their secretly recorded conversations, reveals that the majority saw Jews, Roma (Gypsies), gays and the disabled as "useless mouths" that deserved to die. They expressed particular hatred of the women and children, whom they feared and hated even more than the enemy soldiers because they were the key to continued survival of their people.

Nazi policies on contraception and abortion have been researched by the feminist leader Gloria Steinem. She found them strongly opposed to any choices for women:

> *"Hitler himself, and the Nazi doctrine he created, were unequivocally opposed to any individual right to abortion. In fact, Hitler's National Socialist Movement preached against and punished contraception, homosexuality, women whose main purpose was not motherhood, men who did not prove their manhood by fathering many children - and anything else that failed to serve the need of preserving and expanding the German state. There were tax penalties for being unmarried, payments for childbearing, and the prohibition of contraception and abortion, as well as homosexuality. Those performing terminations faced a possible death penalty. In 1933 feminists were removed from teaching and other public posts by the same law that removed 'non-Aryans' from such jobs."*

She quotes Adolf Hitler himself as the prime advocate of eugenics in Germany:

> *"Every child that a woman brings into the world is a battle, a battle waged for the existence of her people..."*

It is ironic then that advocates of contraception are often accused by the opposition of being eugenicists. In fact it is the pro-natalists who are preaching eugenics in a modern context, often seeking to ban all forms of family planning. Put simply, they are arguing for increases in their own group's population in competition with other groups, perhaps killing the others or forcing them out of their homes and lands. They are also prepared to use their own children as cannon fodder in sectarian conflicts. In a civil war situation they kill children of the "other" side, or abduct those children, brutalise and drug them and force them to fight, and in extreme cases even to commit atrocities against their own people under threat of being killed themselves if they refuse.

For terrorist groups using suicide bombings there have been reports of children being used to carry explosives, often without any understanding of the horror they are involved in. For such people it is only the numbers of children that counts - individuals are expendable. Forced childbirth for women in their own group is the other side of genocide against others. There is tragic evidence from other conflicts that babies and children are seen as targets by some regimes and militias. In Syria, for example, there have been reports of government aircraft deliberately bombing groups of children playing outside the houses. In Myanmar, government troops have deliberately targeted babies and children for killings. In the Central African Republic the Seleka militia groups have killed large numbers of women with children. A first aid worker reported in 2013 that in the village of Bombi Te armed militia first robbed his wife, then ordered her to leave while they attacked her four-year-old child.

> *"They tried to shoot him but the gun was not working. So they slit his throat instead. What threat does this child pose to the Seleka?"*

"Meanwhile, get breeding"

Advocates of forcing women to bear more children are getting louder, and Europe and the US - where most women now have access to a range of contraception - seem to be hotspots for this. Jonathan V Last, the US author of *What to Expect When No One's Expecting*, claims that his people are having "too few babies". He argues::

> *"If America wants to continue to lead the world, we need to have more babies."*

Conservative British commentator Charles Moore wrote:

> *"You can borrow and spend hugely if you know that the generation that will end up with the bill is much larger than your own. If it is much smaller, you can't; but we have. As a result, Europe is a dying business. Most of the world is not. So it is winning... Meanwhile, get breeding."*

There has been a flurry of other overtly racist books published in the United States, some of them best-sellers, which claim that because the "white" population of Europe and North America in particular is not increasing, or not fast enough, they face catastrophe. They claim that people of other religions and "races" will increase their numbers more rapidly and somehow overwhelm the native population. Pat Buchanan, in *The Death of the West*, claims:

> *"The rise of feminism spells the death of the nation and the end of the West."*

Mark Steyn in *America Alone* predicts:

> *"the demise of European races too self-absorbed to breed. In demographic terms, the salient feature of much of the 'progressive agenda' - abortion, gay marriage, endlessly deferred adulthood [means]... as fertility dries up, so do societies."*

This word "breeding" is for domestic animals used for human use, and is completely inappropriate for our fellow-humans.

The numbers they most want to increase are fellow-conservatives. Here is David Bentley Hart, a conservative Catholic theologian in the US:

> *"Probably the most subversive and effective strategy we might undertake would be one of militant fecundity: abundant, relentless, exuberant, and defiant childbearing. Given the reluctance of modern men and women to be fruitful and multiply, it would not be difficult, surely, for the devout to accomplish - in no more than a generation or two - a demographic revolution."*

He is referring to the Catholic Church's expansion in opposition to Protestants, members of other faiths, and non-believers. Perhaps more precisely, since most Catholics now use contraception and have small families, it is a call to use women to grow the militant conservative faction within the church at the expense of the liberals. Membership is seen as a battle of the numbers. Once a Catholic community is established, especially in the developed countries, conversion to the faith is uncommon so church membership will grow almost entirely through the number of babies its members have. This must be an important factor in the hierarchy's insistence on opposing birth planning or choice, and giving this priority over moral issues.

The "get breeding" order might all seem a bit of a joke - a few ultra-conservatives ranting and raving while most people simply ignore what they have to say and make their own decisions. But in many parts of the world it is deadly serious. Many ethnic, cultural and religious rivalries, many of them spilling over into war, are stoked by the perception that "they" are breeding and "we" are not, or at least not fast enough. Since this is very largely a male argument (and since they have not yet worked out how to make babies on their own) it means heavy pressure on girls and women to marry early and face a lifetime of pregnancies and childbirth, while contraception is made unavailable and terminations are made highly dangerous. It is a pattern seen around the world in areas with ongoing conflict.

The "breeding" ideology is particularly dangerous among far-right and racist groups in western countries, who are increasingly the source of terrorist attacks there. Several of these attackers in the last few years have produced long justifications for their actions, which are spread mainly through social media, and these rely heavily on conspiracy theories about the disappearance of "whites" because they are not producing enough children. The suspect in the murderous attack on a mosque in Christchurch, New Zealand, produced a long diatribe referring to these conspiracy theories and entitled "The great replacement," which imagines the displacement of white European people by immigrants of other backgrounds, with the repeated phrase:

"It's the birthrates"
"It's the birthrates"
"It's the birthrates"

"Motherhood as punishment"

Many of the countries with repressive laws against contraception and abortion have a background of ethnic or religious tensions and conflicts. Northern Ireland, for example, with its extreme sensitivities over population numbers of Catholics and Protestants, had an almost total legal ban on abortion for many years until overruled by the UK Parliament. It had a culture of enforced motherhood which came from enforcers on both sides of the religious divide. One pro-choice campaigner in Northern Ireland described the attitudes of many towards women who wanted to terminate an unwanted pregnancy:

> *"There just seems to be this huge culture of shame. This idea that oh, you had sex, you are a dirty slut, the punishment is motherhood."*

As the Peruvian pro-choice activist Kelly Cieza puts it:

> *"Motherhood cannot be imposed as an obligation or punishment."*

Sadly, in too many areas it can be, and it is. How can they use childbirth and the care of a baby as punishment? The answer, presumably, is that they do not care about their real welfare.

The battles over abortion are still raging even in the countries with mainly liberal law and social policy, but the situation is worse - much worse - for women facing the new eugenics being imposed in many developing countries where there is sectarian or religious competition over numbers. In Nigeria, for example, the question of how many people there are, in which region of the country or in which ethnic or religious group, is too sensitive for even a proper census. Politicians of different groups have exploited the fear that "the others" are greater in number, are increasing faster, and therefore will get more resources. The result: very few options for women to plan the birth of their children, high rates of enforced pregnancy and childbirth, and extremely high mortality rates. Overall population numbers have tripled since independence in 1960, and could double again in less than 25 years. As a result of its ethnic conflicts, Nigeria has one of the highest rates of pregnancy and childbirth in the world.

Intense pressure on women to bear more children is also a feature of colonial and settler movements. In the colonisation period in what is now the United States, for example, the settlers' birth rates were exceptionally high - far exceeding those in Europe, from which they had recently arrived. At the same time the numbers of Native Americans were drastically cut by warfare and massacres, disease, destruction of the buffalo on which many depended, and expulsion from their lands. Their numbers east of the Mississippi River fell from an estimated two million in 1492 to just a quarter of a million in 1750 - that is, three quarters of the population died in less than sixty years. The same or similar phenomenon can be found in many expansionist societies today which are seeking to drive out the inhabitants of other groups, whether through violence or by the sheer weight of their own group's numbers.

"A sacrificial role"

The concept of "fundamentalism" is also important here. It was coined as a term for Christian evangelicals in the United States in the early 20th century who were fighting for the "fundamentals of faith" in the face of modern ideas. It can now be applied to a particular use (or abuse) of religion across the whole spectrum. Women's organisations have identified fundamentalist groups in Catholic and other Christian churches, Muslim, Buddhist, Hindu, Jewish and Sikh religions, as well as local ethno-religious traditions such as the

Kenyan Mungiki movement, Mexican indigenous Tepehuan, Nepali shamanism, and new religions or cults such as the Moonies' Unification Church which has arranged involuntary marriages for thousands of its younger members as a way of increasing their numbers.

A fairly typical example of the sectarian attitudes of these groups is from MS Golwalkar, an architect of the "Hindutva" (Hinduness) ideology:

> *"The non-Hindu people of Hindustan must either adopt Hindu culture and language, must learn and respect and hold in reverence the Hindu religion, must entertain no idea but of those of glorification of the Hindu race and culture or may stay in the country wholly subordinated to the Hindu nation, deserving no privileges, far less any preferential treatment - not even citizens' rights."*

A common theme here, and of fundamentalists in general, is a hatred and scorn for the idea of equality for all citizens or of universal human rights, and particularly women's rights.

With the exception of some cults, the fundamentalists do not represent their whole religion. They operate a distortion of their faith which they claim to be "the Truth". While fundamentalists of different groups disagree violently with each other and are in conflict on many issues, a common theme among them is controlling "their" women, and especially pregnancies and childbearing, in order to maximise the number of "their" children. A militantly male phenomenon (although women can be co-opted), it represents both a backlash against the women's movement, and a distancing or even contempt among the men involved for all women, our bodies, feelings and wishes.

The Anglican commentator Reverend Giles Fraser,

who often has to deal with Christian Protestant fundamentalists, describes them as:

> *"locked in a self-referencing worldview where truth is about strict internal coherence rather than any reaching out to reality,"*

It might be described as an extreme authoritarianism. Their logic is: I have authority over everyone else, especially the women, because I can claim these sacred texts and ancient traditions. These are absolute and not open to question or discussion. Therefore my orders cannot be questioned, and certainly not by those women.

It is an individual pathology which is translated into a demand for implacable loyalty to the group and to themselves. As one feminist from Argentina has put it,

> *"Speaking with the support of God is something very different from speaking without it... It puts [women] on the side of sin and the Devil."*

Nira Yuval-Davis, an observer of the phenomenon in conservative Judaism, calls it "a political use of religion".

> *"This version of religion, because it tends to be pre-modern and talk about 'purification' and going back to the 'Truth', latches on to patriarchal modes of society and control of women."*

She adds that some women in the Israeli settler movement take it on themselves as a patriotic or religious duty to have as many children as possible.

> *"The role of the mother is absolutely central, in a kind of sacrificial role for the settlement,"*

Meanwhile the late Palestinian leader Yasser Arafat described his biggest weapon as:

> *"the womb of the Arab woman".*

In the context of the Arab-Israeli conflict all this would be farcical if it were not so tragic in terms of human lives and any prospect of peace.

A Muslim cleric in Iran, Mojtaba Takhtipour, interviewed by the *New York Times*, said that Islam orders a quest for a perfect society.

"That means we need to increase the number of Muslims, so we also need more kids."

To those who worry about supporting large numbers of children, he argues:

"We do believe that ultimately God will provide our daily bread. So go out and have kids and have faith, is what I always say."

This is far from the accepted view throughout Islam, but since there is no central religious authority for the faith, unlike the Catholic and other churches, there can be many different authorities and interpretations.

Ancient and modern

Feminist observers of fundamentalism see it not as some genuine survival from pre-modern times but as a very modern reaction to events in the world today, and especially the fight for resources. Most fundamentalists, they argue, are not really retreating into the past: they use modern technologies to spread their message including the internet, cable TV and satellite communications. They also operate transnationally, using modern media, often to bypass the opposition they may face at home.

The Association for Women's Rights in Development (AWID) has surveyed 1,600 women's rights activists facing fundamentalist opposition. They conclude that the fundamentalists are extremely right-wing politically, absolutist and intolerant, with:

> "*a conviction that they are divinely mandated to impose on others what they believe to be the singular truth*".

Not all fundamentalist groups are violent, but those that are will not hesitate to attack other people, either verbally or sometimes with the threat or use of force. The main targets are likely to be members of other groups and other religions, or none, while people within their own community may also be subject to pressure if they refuse to accept their ideas. Extreme fundamentalists will often attack their own co-religionists precisely because they have little real depth of support within the community. A human rights activist from Egypt told AWID researchers:

> "*In most cases when people are offered an alternative interpretation, they take it, because they say it's a suffocating life to live as is preached by those religious fundamentalists.*"

The position of the Catholic hierarchy also comes to mind, where they have failed to convince their own members on "Life" issues but devote great efforts to persuading politicians nationally and internationally to block women's rights, for Catholics and non-Catholics alike, and especially on fertility.

The AWID study concludes that among fundamentalists,

> "*women are conceptualized as the reproducers and symbols of a community's collective identity, and therefore of its influence and power.*"

This translates into an obsession with the control of women's bodies and autonomy, with particular emphasis on restricting choice about having children, imposing a strict "morality" on women, and a rigid definition of women's and men's roles in the family and society. Many of them are hostile to sexual non-conformists such as lesbians, gay men and transsexuals, as well as women and girls who defy their rules. In Mongolia for example there are increasing threats coming from ultra-nationalist groups and religious fundamentalists to stop abortion, which is currently legal, claiming that women should produce more babies to ensure national security and sustain the so-called "pure Mongolian blood." In Thailand, it is militant Buddhist fundamentalists taking a similar line. The pattern is repeated in many other countries across the world.

Most fundamentalists are actively recruiting, especially among young and disaffected people who are looking for a cause and an identity. Many of them specialise in offering education and the attractions of their youth organisations. Their absolutist message can be very appealing to young people, especially boys and men who are seeking a strong identity for themselves, some power over women, and a role and purpose in society; they can then be mobilised for the cause. In this way AWID describes fundamentalists, where they are strong, as:

> *"effectively influencing society without having to capture state power"*.

Is this war?

The fundamentalists of all major religions are of course competing with each other to recruit more and more members, especially in areas with sectarian tensions. With both sides trying to increase their numbers by persuading or forcing the women to have big families, there can be a kind of arms race of childbirth. In the Middle East generally, there is increasing conflict between Sunnis, the majority who also have the highest birth rate, and Shias who generally have much smaller families. Da'esh (ISIS), which is Sunni-based, have put great efforts into using the internet to groom and recruit Muslim women from other countries to travel to occupied areas to marry their fighters and produce as many babies as possible. They have also kidnapped enormous numbers of Yazidi and other women from areas they have occupied and subjected them to systematic rape, sale as sex slaves, and forcing them to bear children for their controllers.

Competition for numbers has been suggested as the real reason for the Catholic hierarchy's emphasis on so-called "Life" issues. For centuries they have had a vigorous missionary effort to set up new churches in Latin America, the Philippines and other areas of the developing world. Since the Reformation in Europe they have had increasing rivalry with the Protestants over their numbers. They now face intense competition with the rapidly growing US-based evangelical churches, especially in Latin America. Some of these evangelicals are themselves fundamentalists who promote conventional domestic roles for women, which would of course include producing many children and bringing them up within an ever-expanding church.

At the same time all religious fundamentalists are competing for recruits with secular movements such as left-wing political parties or other opposition groups. In the many totalitarian countries which cannot tolerate any opposition, political parties have been savagely repressed and this has left the field clear for the religious movements. In many cases these survive and thrive in poor areas by offering basic medical or welfare services - but strictly no family planning.

The condition of any help, of course, is loyalty to them and at least a passive acceptance of their doctrines.

Fundamentalists have always been with us, if only as a personality type which demands that they know best, and how dare you question them? What is new in the modern world is the political clout they have accumulated, especially as they use modern mass media and form alliances with conservative and nationalist forces. Many of them are well-funded, and may have great influence over governments. Fundamentalist Christians and the "Tea Party" movement in the US scored a major victory with the election of Donald Trump as President. Variations on this theme can be found, among many others, with Catholic hierarchies in the Philippines and much of Latin America, Buddhist fundamentalists in Myanmar (Burma), Da'esh (ISIS), al-Qa'ida and allied Islamist groups controlling whole areas in the Middle East, Somalia and parts of West Africa, or Hindu fundamentalists attacking Muslims in India or Muslims attacking religious minorities in Pakistan.

In extreme cases sectarian fundamentalists will use violence, up to and including murder, to silence criticism especially from human rights workers. Several women defenders of human rights have been killed or badly hurt by fundamentalists. Nearly 10% of women's rights activists have experienced attacks on their offices or theft of their equipment, according to the AWID survey.

This violence has sometimes been turned on non-political humanitarian organisations, especially health workers. Vaccination campaigns against polio have been a particular target. In northern Nigeria, for example, at least nine women were shot dead while working on a programme to immunise children against polio, and several doctors were also murdered. This was blamed on the Islamist militia group Boko Haram. The campaign against immunisation is linked to claims by some Imams that the drops are contaminated, as part of a "western campaign" to sterilise young girls and supposedly to wipe out the whole Muslim population.

The result of this and other attacks and scares was an epidemic of polio which led to hundreds of children being infected, many dying of polio and others being so severely disabled that they can only survive by begging in the streets. This was at a time when the disease had been eliminated from almost every other country in the world. India, for example, has achieved a complete eradication of polio after an exhaustive campaign. More recently, strenuous efforts to immunise children across Nigeria have been successful, with that country also declared free of the disease in 2020.

"It's a Muslim man's duty"

Polio eradication campaigns and health services are also targets for Islamists in the Peshawar area of Pakistan. Eight health workers were killed there in a single week in 2013, including those taking part in an ambitious drive to immunise millions of children against polio. This followed claims by the Taliban that the anti-polio work was part of a western plot to sterilise women.

At the heart of the conflict in Pakistan are Lady Health Workers (LHWs), a force of 110,000 women set up by the late Benazir Bhutto, when she was Prime Minister, to help women and children. They are specifically tasked with visiting women at home to provide general health and contraceptive services, since many are not allowed to visit clinics on their own.

These health workers became a prime target for Taliban and other Islamist groups in Pakistan, with threats of kidnapping, rape and in some cases murder. The most intimidating tactic is to "name and shame" individual women working in health, using radio broadcasts to issue fatwas against them personally. These declared that "it is a Muslim man's duty" to kidnap the women health workers when they paid home visits, to force them into marriages even if they were already married, or to use them as sexual slaves. In the Swat region, which the Taliban occupied for three years up to 2009, their chief Maulana Fazlullah even declared LHWs to be "fit for murder". Some were indeed executed, publicly beaten, or their family members were murdered.

The threats against LHWs in Swat understandably forced many of them to resign, stop working or flee the area, and their patients suffered badly as a result. A study by the British Medical Journal found an increased number of deaths in childbirth, forced marriages and dangerous abortions. They quote one supervisor:

> *"A lot of people stopped using family planning methods. They said it's against Islam. They got pregnant. Now the Taliban are gone they are aborting the pregnancies. Abortions are on the rise and women are dying."*

Horrifying as this is, it is important to note that Islamist paranoia about health workers has been increased by incidents where western military units, including special forces, have hidden behind health and other aid projects. This has increased suspicion of all aid projects and made it much more dangerous for them to do their work. US special forces set up a "dummy" polio immunisation scheme as cover for their tracking and murder of al-Qa'ida chief Osama bin Laden. The damage done by this to health programmes, especially for women, has been enormous and the tactic cannot be justified. It is essential that all military forces stop using health and aid programmes as cover for their own activities. It will take a long time for trust in health outreach work to be fully restored. We are seeing the often fatal consequences of this distrust with the vaccine refusal fuelling the worldwide Covid-19 pandemic.

Pakistan had previously been a pioneer of family planning, the second country (after India) ever to initiate a national service. Fundamentalists have now managed to entrench the idea, especially in rural areas, that using contraception is "un-Islamic", and as a result many of the people have stopped using it and the country is now one of the least successful in offering services.

> *"Family planning is a Western ideology to stop women from giving birth completely,"*

one Islamist told BBC News. Almost all the women in Pakistan who use modern contraception now are urban and educated, while those most in need of the services have little or no access.

Vote banks

This is in stark contrast to the fact that some of the most successful countries in this field - notably Iran, Bangladesh and Indonesia - are Muslim-majority states, with strong Islamic government identities. One important factor is that they have religious parties which have more enlightened attitudes, for example the Jamaat in Bangladesh which has no policy of opposing choice. They are among those who accept the original teachings of Islam: there is consensus among scholars that neither Quranic verses nor the Hadith contain any instructions on contraception. In fact Muslim governments have historically allowed contraception and abortion, for example in the Ottoman Empire and in Egypt. As with historical Catholic thought, it was believed that the foetus did not undergo "ensoulment" to become a human being until 120 days after conception

In Pakistan what appears to be a religious issue may be better described as political, with a struggle for influence between different groups. Two major Islamic political parties, JUI-F and Jamaat-e-Islami, have opposed choice since the 1930s. As Dr Mehtab Karim has pointed out, the "vote bank" for the hard-line Islamic parties will increase from about 85 million people in 2013 to over 105 million in the next five years because of their pro-natalist policies. Almost all of these people will be very poor and illiterate: perfect voting fodder to maintain and increase hard-line political influence and bring them to power.

Similar calculations seem to underlie the position of other Islamist parties and some Islamist governments, where political power rests on the number of their supporters. For example the Muslim Brotherhood, when in power in Egypt, denounced the proposed "Agreed Conclusions" of the UN Commission on the Status of Women, which called for sexual and reproductive rights for women, as "the intellectual and cultural invasion of Muslim countries" which would undermine Islamic ethics and "destroy the family". Many women's groups, clerics and scholars in Islamic countries are contesting such fundamentalist dictates, often at considerable personal risk. During the Arab Spring uprising and subsequent protests in Egypt women played a key role, coming out in huge numbers to demonstrate for a democratic future. They were targeted by organised gangs of men who picked out women for sexual assault and rape, often leading to severe injuries.

These men were identified as Muslim Brotherhood members and Salafists operating systematically: around 15-20 men would surround one or two women, then up to 50 men would join in. The inner group would strip, molest and rape the women, and the outer group would fight off anyone trying to rescue them. Under Morsi's Muslim Brotherhood government no action was taken to prevent these assaults and no arrests or prosecutions undertaken, even where the perpetrators were identified. Indeed, there were incidents where the security forces helped the Islamists hold on to their "captured women". Was this a war against women? Apparently, for the Islamists, it was.

Women activists around the world are bravely confronting fundamentalists of all stripes. One of many examples is Musarrat Shaheen, a tribal woman and former film star from the DI Khan area near the Afghan border, which is plagued by extremist violence. Standing for election to the national parliament in Pakistan, she was contemptuous of the male religious leaders - a feeling that stems from her time as a family planning adviser in the 1970s. She told reporters:

> *"I had to travel alone going door to door and these mullahs would tell people to beat me up with a stick. They got me sacked because I was unmarried."*

She and other women stood successfully for election in 2013 to show that women could have a say in their own future and could get elected, despite the threats.

"Giving birth is a patriotic duty"

Religious fundamentalism is not the only factor in campaigns against contraception. Nationalism, too, can come into play. Two examples are from the former Soviet bloc in Eastern Europe. In Romania under Nicolae Ceausescu, contraception and abortion were banned in order to force women to have babies they often could not feed, clothe or house. Ceausescu announced:

> *"The foetus is the socialist property of the whole society. Giving birth is a patriotic duty… Those who refuse to have children are deserters."*

The result was great misery, with the highest maternal mortality rates in Europe. 87% of the deaths were the result of dangerous abortions. Large numbers of babies and children were abandoned in State orphanages which were filthy and hugely overcrowded, and care was rudimentary at best. A movement arose among childless couples in western countries to adopt these "orphans" (although their parents were often still alive and living nearby). Many of the children suffered permanent illness and disability as a result of the physical and emotional neglect they had suffered.

The other example was the former Soviet Union, where contraceptives were almost impossible to get but abortions were freely offered at government clinics, and frequent abortions were the only way for most women to prevent unwanted births. These operations were often done without anaesthetic, a form of torture that seemed to be a punishment for not producing a baby for the Motherland. The Soviets had suffered huge losses of both soldiers and civilians in the Second World War and were trying to encourage large families through withholding contraception, a "childless" tax, and medals and rewards for Hero Mothers who had large families. The policy simply did not work in towns and cities because women were unable to look after babies and children while doing their obligatory full-time jobs, and living in overcrowded shared flats. They were very unwilling to leave children in the State nurseries which - apart from those catering for the elite - were inadequate and even dangerous.

There are countries where the population is declining, including probably modern Russia although the statistics on this have been questioned. The most important cause of declining population numbers is out-migration, in situations where the prospects for younger people are simply better elsewhere. Their own children will probably be born and live permanently in other countries. This applies mainly in Eastern and Southern Europe, with migration to Western Europe, together with Cuba and Puerto Rico, both losing people to the US. By 2030 it is predicted that falling numbers will also apply to Japan, Thailand, Italy, Greece and Spain, based on current fertility and migration levels. It is striking that a slight fall in numbers, following an enormous increase, is leading to loud complaints by some governments who see this as some kind of threat to their very survival. The Government of China is just the latest to press the panic button because its population growth rate has slowed to just above replacement level.

Putting pressure on people to have more children, when they know they cannot care for them, simply does not work but merely produces misery. In western Europe between the two world wars, after the huge losses of men during the First World War, many governments had pro-natalist policies which included State subsidies for extra babies. Yet with an economic depression, unemployment, poverty and poor housing, people could not afford to have many children and did whatever they could to avoid or terminate pregnancy. Birth rates fell rapidly, even though contraception at that time was far less good than today's (many relied on the withdrawal method) and abortion was illegal.

My own grandparents were caught up in this dilemma: they both worked for an institution which provided their food, but not their children's - they had to pay per child out of their meagre wages. When a "surprise" third child arrived he had to be hidden away when inspectors came.

If people had sex outside marriage at that time men were under no obligation to support any children that resulted. Women were literally "left holding the baby," as it was described, and subjected to the great shame of illegitimacy - hence the desperation to "get rid of it" and the high levels of extremely dangerous abortions, or the many young women – estimated at a quarter of a million – having their babies taken away for adoption by others.

In many situations governments, religious fund-amentalists and nationalist or sectarian movements are able to force people to have children through their public campaigns, putting up barriers to family planning and sometimes personal threats. These too are driven by men who take little or no personal responsibility for looking after the extra children they help to create. In some cases they distort the truth about human bodies with outrageous fictions. Some Catholic organisations, for instance, misrepresent contraceptives as "really" abortion, or claim dangers from terminations ("abortion causes cancer") which do not exist. Meanwhile some ultra-conservatives in the United States openly justify rape, and enforced childbirth if that is the result. Some have made startling claims that women "raped easy," would not resist an attack but only call it rape the next morning, and that in any case it could not have been rape if the woman became pregnant. Babies that resulted from a rape would be "God's gifts". Or should that be: My God's punishment on godless you?

"Family planning is a pro-life cause"

If religious fundamentalists and nationalists would only devote their attention to the real welfare of their communities, including the care and upbringing of children, and if they insisted on the responsibilities of men, there might be some justification for their wanting more children. If only they would campaign for a genuinely moral approach, and against exploitative and violent behaviour in relationships, they might acquire moral credibility. A Catholic priest quoted by the journalist Chris Hedges has it about right:

> "Faith always starts with oneself. It means an overriding sense of responsibility for the universe, making sure that universe is left in good hands…"

It is important to remember that the fundamentalists do not represent mainstream religious approaches, although they often claim to do so. Nor are all conservatives necessarily on the wrong side. Many faith-based organisations are working quietly but effectively to promote safe sex, contraception, and sometimes abortion as well. Meanwhile, let us conclude with the comment of a US evangelical Christian and conservative columnist, Michael Gerson, who saw this work on the ground in rural areas of the Democratic Republic of Congo. Speaking at a conference in 2013 after the visit he said:

> *"[Family planning] is often a controversial topic here in [Washington] DC, but it shouldn't be. When births are spaced more than 24 months apart, both mothers and children are dramatically more likely to survive. In cases like this, family planning is a pro-life cause, and everyone should support it."*

Resources

Michelle Goldberg, *The Great Population Panic" in The Means of Reproduction: Sex, Power and the Future of the World* (Penguin Press, New York, 2009).

Mark Steyn, *America Alone: The End of the World As We Know It* (Regnery Publishing, Washington DC, 2006).

Pat Buchanan, *The Death of the West: How Dying Populations and Immigrant Invasions Imperil Our Country and Civilization* (St Martin's Press, New York, 2002).

Sonke Neitzel and Harald Welzer, *Soldaten: On Fighting, Killing and Dying*, (Simon & Schuster, 2013).

TV Channel Five (UK), "Children of the Master Race," 21 November 2013.

Gloria Steinem, article in *Speak Out Against the New Right*, edited by Herbert F. Vetter (Boston: Beacon Press, 1982).

Jonathan V Last, *What to Expect When No-one's Expecting* (Encounter Books, 2013).

GISA: Global Interfaith and Secular Alliance, convened by Catholics for Choice and the Asian-Pacific Resource & Research Centre for Women.

Association for Women's Rights in Development (AWID): papers on fundamentalism: "New Insights on Religious Fundamentalisms, Research Highlights," September 2009, and "Exposed: Ten Myths About Religious Fundamentalisms," by Cassandra Balchin, November 2008

Dr Mehtab S Karim, "Population Bomb", The News, Pakistan, 6 April 201.

Ziba Mir-Hosseini and others (eds): *Gender and Equality in Muslim Family Law: Justice and Ethics in the Islamic Legal Tradition*, IB Tauris, London, 2013.

"How the Taliban undermined community healthcare in Swat, Pakistan," by Iftikhar Ud Din and others, British Medical Journal, 21 March 2012.

Sneha Barot, "A Common Cause: Faith-Based Organizations and Promoting Access to Family Planning in the Developing World," Guttmacher Policy Review, Fall 2013, Volume 16, Number 4.

Chapter four

AN "AGEING SOCIETY"? DON'T PANIC!

In the richer countries there are regular loud claims that they are in an "ageing society" and this is often used to justify claims that everybody must have more children. Ageing is terrible, they cry. It's not even normal! This conjures up for me Oscar Wilde's short story, "The Picture of Dorian Gray". A beautiful young man is haunted by his own portrait, even though it is hidden away in the attic. This picture ages rapidly and within days it moves to a hideous old age, decay and death, revealing his own corruption and his hideous future.

> "What the worm was to the corpse, his sins would be to the painted image on the canvas. They would mar its beauty and eat away its grace. They would defile it and make it shameful. And yet the thing would live on. It would be always alive."

In the end the picture does show him dead.

> "Suddenly, time stopped for him. Yes, that blind, slow-breathing thing crawled no more, and horrible thoughts, time

> *being dead, raced nimbly on in front, and dragged a hideous*
> *future from its grave, and showed it to him. He stared at it. Its*
> *very horror made him stone."*

This is one of the very few stories ever written that, in an age-obsessed world, directly addresses our desperate longing to hold on to our youth, and our fear of getting older even though it starts at birth and continues throughout our lives. I would have to look back at my own teenage self to confess that I too, as a young person, wondered what those grey-looking older people were for, and even had the fleeting thought that they might as well die soon. Now I am older, I finally understand what older people are for...

Dorian Gray syndrome seems to lie behind much of the discussion among politicians and demographers about the "ageing society" and how awful that must be (especially as they are themselves approaching this category, or are already there). The solution they put forward, all too often, is:more babies! Now! Get breeding, quick... never mind if it is so unsafe that some die before they even start working for us, we'll just get more. Make sure those women give us young people to provide more cheap labour, so there will be plenty of them to look after us oldies and keep us alive and kicking as long as possible. Why should we care about their future? They will get older too, but we will be dead by then.

"China will lose its edge"

There are many other countries where panic is apparently rising over their supposedly "ageing society", fostered strangely by the United Nations and its agencies. A report from the UN children's agency Unicef in 2012 claims:

"The global old-age dependency rate will accelerate markedly, almost tripling from 12% in 2010 to around 32% in 2070." Some agencies define "old" as over 60 but the retirement age is below that in several countries – in China it is currently 50 for women in manual work and 55 for white-collar employees. According to current UN definitions a country may officially become "an ageing society" when people 60 years of age or older account for 10% of the total population. Unicef defines it as 65 and above, but also assumes that older people are inevitably dependent on younger ones. There is no subtlety here, no recognition of older people's role in the community as a whole. "Old age dependency" seems to be an article of faith for Unicef and other agencies, and we are wicked consumers of "essential resources" that should be going to more and more children. Perhaps they will be calling us witches next, with special reference to those difficult women who manage to live longer than men. So the witch must die?

In 2021 the Government of China pressed the panic button because of falling birth rates. In fact the population was still increasing, although slowly. Ning Jizhe, head of its National Bureau of Statistics, has argued that the panic is misplaced: China's large population base has not changed, he commented, and the advantage of its large domestic market and plentiful labour force would exist "for a long time." Despite fears of the "ageing population", in fact China's average age, at 38.8, is similar to that of the US. It seems that nationalism is at work in the fear of population stability, with many predicting that its numbers will be overtaken by those of India. It is hard to see how this would disadvantage China, unless of course they just want enormous numbers of young people in the labour force to be exploited by keeping wages low. The website *China* Power sums it up:

> *"This trend [of longer life expectancy and more older people] is particularly worrisome for China, as its development is tied to its demographic advantages. For decades, China reaped the benefits of a demographic dividend that supplied a young workforce for its manufacturing sector, which enabled China to emerge as a global economic power."*

A leading Chinese official, Lou Jiwei, arguing for lifting the "one child" policy, saw it very much in the same terms:

> *"The Chinese population is aging and labor costs are increasing. Without due measures, China will lose its edge over other countries."*

Professor Cai Fang, direction of the Institute of Population and Labor Economics, has argued that as a result of its "one child" policy China was losing its "demographic dividends" as ageing had accelerated and the dependency ratio (the number of children and the elderly compared to working-age adults) had stopped declining in 2011. His conclusion: to "get" more children. The limit has now been raised from one to three children per family.

The complexity of real lives

Let us get back to the real world, where older people have a crucial role in supporting those who really are dependent, often at great cost to themselves. Many are in the workforce, earning money or helping the younger members of the family or community. They may be caring for others, with many of them bringing up grandchildren when parents work elsewhere, die or become sick and disabled. Many older people do unpaid voluntary work in the community. In the process, they are saving huge amounts of money in care costs that would otherwise fall to local and national governments. Perhaps Unicef disapproves of all the older people who feed and look after children? The thought is bizarre. In Britain alone, research by Carers UK shows the economic value of work by carers is a massive £119 billion a year, and growing rapidly. This is bigger than the total budget of the National Health Service. If you are working long hours to care unpaid for a dependent person, is it not an insult to describe you as a dependant?

There are indeed massive changes in the age structure of populations almost everywhere in the world, but the biggest change of all is the increasing numbers of children and young people in the poorer countries, while a much smaller trend is more adults living beyond 60 or 65 in the richer ones. Both of these trends are the result of the same phenomenon: successful campaigns to improve people's health and survival rates. They are a necessary element in the transition from many births and many deaths to a greatly reduced mortality for everyone, in practically all countries. You would find it hard to find a demographer or politician who wanted to bring back population control by death as an instrument of policy, so therefore they have to accept that there will be imbalances in the age structure if we hope to move towards a stable and balanced population, as well as a healthier one. Panic attacks over the "ageing society" and "dependency ratios" merely obstruct the move towards this goal.

It is quite wrong to count people as "economically productive" or "dependents" based purely on their age. The reality is far more complex. Let us remember that many older people - and children too - contribute to household incomes. At the same time there are increasing numbers of sick and disabled people who survive childhood, especially in poor regions and countries, to become dependent on others while of "working age" - not through their choice but often because of discrimination in their own societies, and lack of the health care and equipment available in richer countries. Meanwhile many able-bodied young people, who should be entering the workforce and helping to maintain themselves and their families, also remain economically dependent because of enormously high levels of unemployment. The number of jobs, and the availability of land and other assets, is far below the numbers entering what should be a "working age".

Getting younger every day

When people live to a greater age they also increase what is described as a "healthy life expectancy," which is the number of years lived in good health. This means that in countries with growing life expectancy people in their 60s, 70s and older are fitter and healthier than their counterparts a generation or two ago, because of better nutrition, medical treatments, and living conditions. This better health is perhaps the greatest change that has happened in the wealthier countries as far as older people are concerned. It undermines the near-panic shown by governments over the "ageing society".

An excellent demolition of the notion of an "ageing population" as some kind of problem is offered by Jeroen Spijker and John MacInnes, who looked in detail at the situation in Britain. They argued that the conventional "old age dependency ratio" is a poor measure of real dependency:

"The population of 2009, despite being much older as measured by years lived, was nevertheless younger than that of 1900 in terms of years left. This is crucial, because many behaviours and attitudes (including those related to health) are more strongly linked to remaining life expectancy than to age … rising life expectancy makes these older people 'younger,' healthier, and fitter than their peers in earlier cohorts."

Their cut-off point is 15 years or less of life expectancy. Most acute medical care costs, they add, occur in the final months of life, and the age at which this occurs has little relevance. So a disadvantaged young person who cannot survive long is really "older" than someone with many more years on the clock who is fit and well.

They also have some challenging thoughts on the so-called "working age" population, where there have been huge changes in recent years. In countries with longer life expectancy, numbers of pensioners have been kept down by raising the age at which people can claim. Young people now start working much later, because of the growth of higher education, while many older workers either retire earlier or later than a fixed age. Meanwhile, greater sex equality and dual-earner families have added five million women workers to the British labour market over the past 50 years. Retired people do not even make up the majority of people who are out of the workforce.

"If we count people who are not employed, for whatever reason, as dependent we find that there are more dependants of working age (9.5 million) than there are older people who do not work."

These are powerful trends moving in opposite directions and

making a nonsense of the old assumptions about who should be considered to be of "working age".

> *"We calculated what we call the real elderly dependency ratio as the sum of men and women with a remaining life expectancy of 15 years or less divided by the number of people in employment. When we use this as a measure, dependency has fallen by one third over the past four decades."*

So much for the panic over increased dependency through "ageing". The rates are also very variable among the richer countries. The United States has a lower ratio than the UK, while in Germany and Italy the real elderly dependency ratio has been almost flat for two decades. Only Japan, which is unusual in having a combination of relatively low birth rates with very little immigration and few women in the labour force, has seen its ratio rise rapidly.

Conflict entrepreneurs

In poorer countries and regions the real dependency issue is the "youth bulge", where survival rates of the children have improved greatly while births have remained at a high level. Many of the young people in this cohort are forced to be dependent on others while scraping a half-living in bits of casual work, some turning to crime, gangs and terrorist organisations to survive, and many girls forced to enter sex work with all its dangers and abuses. Unemployed young people from rural areas are moving in huge numbers to informal settlements in towns and cities, which are already massively overcrowded. Some of them face death as they cross oceans or climb frontier fences to a perhaps illusory promised land in a richer country. If anything, this generation will face even worse problems as more and more teenagers swell the ranks of the supposedly "working-aged" - young people for whom there is little work and no livelihood.

The best way to help the armies of unemployed young people, and the children coming up behind them, would be to help women reduce the numbers of babies being born now. In about 15 years' time these new babies would compete with and perhaps undercut them in the battle for jobs, land, food, water, education, housing, health care and even survival itself.

The consequences of all this are apparent in most of the "youth bulge" countries. In Mexico, for example, as described by Pedro Salazar Ugarte, writing in the *Boston Review* about the violence and instability afflicting his country despite its being one of the fastest-growing economies:

> *"Mexico… may take off or it may collapse. And I do not exaggerate or mean this rhetorically. Never before has Mexico had so many young people: nearly 30 million men and women aged 15-29, representing 26.4% of the country's population. They are what we call in Mexico the 'demographic bonus,' at first considered a great opportunity to enhance the country's growth and development, and now a threat to its existence. Millions of them have been excluded from these key social institutions: learning and work. Young men and women, Mexico's future, are being left without futures of their own… If Mexico does not guarantee its young people a fair chance at success, it can expect a violent future."*

Mexico is indeed already suffering huge problems of gang violence. This is also the conclusion that David Kilcullen comes to in his survey of urban unrest in many rapidly growing coastal cities, especially in the developing world.

> *"A megacity under stress can offer opportunities for conflict entrepreneurs (gang leaders, crime bosses or militant extremists) to control populations, provided they create a predictable rule set that makes people feel safe in the face of instability… whether people like the group or not, and regardless of the content of those rules. Eventually… it may gain the loyalty and support of the local population."*

Although he describes this in fairly neutral terms, we are talking about organisations which aim to take over control of areas by means of protection and extortion rackets: pay our percentage, sell our drugs, and above all keep quiet about what you know. Otherwise your family's livelihood could be destroyed, and you and your relations could be killed.

Terror

This is a system of organised terror that, once entrenched, is very hard for a democratic government to control. Italy's Mafia and 'Ndrangheta crime groups are well-known examples. They grew up over centuries of shifting colonial conquest and occupation, with weak local governments, and are bigger than ever now with their shift to drug dealing, people trafficking, prostitution and crime generally which now extends world-wide. There are many criminal gangs in other countries which have national and international reach, starting in different local areas which all had the common feature of a lack of central authority and no alternative livelihood for many young people. The pirates based in lawless Somalia, who have been hijacking shipping and demanding huge ransoms for kidnap victims, are just one of the better-known examples.

Another example of this is urban Kenya, where the National Crime Research Centre has identified at least 46 criminal gangs, some of them as violent as the al-Shabaab group which attacked the Westgate shopping centre in Nairobi. These gangs have come to dominate the city's shanty towns, which account for more than 60% of Nairobi's population. Kilcullen argues that with an expected three billion new urban-dwellers expected to arrive in the megacities by the middle of this century, the disruption by gangs and crime bosses could be even greater than the threat of terrorism from extremist Islamist groups. Finding community solutions to these problems, he adds, could be impossible

> *"when the community is under threat and someone is shooting at you."*

The situation arises not only from the sheer numbers, but also of course from the extreme inequality of opportunity and wealth which is a characteristic of most developing countries, especially those with the highest economic growth rates. Nigeria is another example of these two factors coming together: its 5.7% fertility rate is among the highest in the world, and already acting as a fierce brake on development in spite of the wealth generated by oil production, which ends up in the hands of a privileged few. Professor Oladapo Ladipo explains that it is hard to grow the economy because of the high dependency, especially of children, and the consequences for their cash-starved parents.

> *"Because you are spending all of your money just trying to help these dependents survive… then you do not have any money left over to invest in economic activities, business, and more education."*

Poverty can also spark conflict if there are disproportionate numbers of landless and unemployed young people. Journalists reporting on the sudden outbreak of sectarian violence between Christians and Muslims in the Central African Republic have reported that young men who suddenly got access to a Kalashnikov rifle, although there were no previous sectarian conflicts, would use it to threaten or kill their neighbours and seize their homes, land and whatever possessions they had. It is a pattern which has been seen in all too many countries around the world.

Who are you calling dependent?

Demographers are finding it hard to include all these considerations in their definition of dependency. They define it simply as "ageing", largely because that is easy to measure - at least in countries which have reasonable records of births and deaths. Unfortunately this easy route presents a badly distorted picture of who in the population is economically productive, and who is really a dependant. It fails to count all those adults of working age who are forced to be dependent on others. To bring this waste of human talent and human energy into the statistics would transform population policies around the world.

So this is my suggestion: use selective sampling alongside national statistics to more accurately define dependency ratios. The work would involve judgments of how to allocate individuals and families living complex lives, and with varying degrees of support and dependency. In poor communities these relationships, complicated as they are, need to be better understood. I suggest these categories.

Economically active

- Employed and self-employed

This category would include all those working in regular jobs, full- or part-time, or running a regular business (for example selling goods or offering services).

- Farmers and agricultural workers

Farmers (including subsistence farmers) would be prominent in this group, with women playing a particularly important role. A large part of their income is in kind rather than money, in the form of food in particular, but most of them are also able to earn a little cash which is essential for sending children to school, clothing, transport, medical care and other items.

- Casual workers

This would particularly cover the huge numbers of people, especially in poor countries, who have no land of their own and no regular jobs or business, but are essential earners nonetheless. They could be running micro-enterprises in street trading, labouring, dressmaking or other casual work, or for huge numbers of women there is sex work. In many cases these would be bringing in the cash on which whole families would have to survive.

- Retired and self-sufficient

These would be people over retirement age who are not financially dependent on family members. Some would still be earning, and many have their own pensions or other income. They may also give financial or practical help to younger family members.

- Essential carers

This is the group of people who may not be economically active in cash terms, but who make a crucial contribution to families, society as a whole, and the economy. They may be assisting working family members and others, or they may provide essential care for ill and disabled people, mainly in their own families. Huge numbers of older people, previously considered to be "dependants", would come into this category. In developing countries with no social services, pensions or benefits system, many older people - mainly women - would be keeping others going, including for example looking after the children of wage-earners, or providing them with food and other essentials. There is usually no cash payment involved.

Some kind of estimate of the value of this work would be extremely useful, even though exact numbers may be hard to come by. In Britain, a report from the insurer RIAS in 2012 calculated that 5.8 million grandparents were regularly looking after children, providing a cash saving in childcare of nearly £11 billion a year. In relative terms the value is likely to be even higher in poorer countries, particularly in countries like the Philippines with high out-migration, where wage-earners may have to move to other countries to support their family and leave their children behind with their grandparents or other relatives.

Economic dependants

- Dependent children

Children up to the age of 15, but with a reduction to reflect the extent to which children are economically active. High proportions of children, especially in developing countries, are contributing financially to their families or simply scraping a living on their own. This obviously applies to abandoned or orphaned street children, but it also involves the legions of children living with their own families who are earning, often in domestic service, manufacturing, street selling and begging. There is also a very high level of contribution by children in farming and labouring families, especially in rural areas. Children also very often look after younger brothers and sisters.

- Dependent adults

People unable to work: would of course include many older people, but only if they are true dependants rather than classified on the basis of age alone. There would also be sick and disabled people who would of course include "working-age" adults, and this would help to draw attention to the extremely high level of disability in many poorer countries resulting from malnutrition and preventable disease. It also arises from injuries suffered by mothers and babies at birth, the result of unintended, closely spaced pregnancies, inadequate nutrition and poor health systems.

- Dependent unemployed

This is a key dependency element which would describe the enormous numbers of young people who are not needed to work within the family, and cannot find a job or other livelihood elsewhere. This category would highlight the problem of unemployment among the "youth bulge" and help to focus the attention of politicians on the issue of how their people need to live rather than merely existing. This category is in fact quite difficult to measure: sample surveys would be needed to assess the numbers of truly unemployed and unproductive people. There is often no absolute dividing line: unemployed people may turn to occasional casual work or street trading when they can, or in desperation may turn to drug dealing, sex work and theft to relieve their dependent or destitute state.

- Criminals

These can be considered to be dependants in the "grey economy": It could be argued that theft, dealing in drugs and other anti-social activity is much worse than being a "dependant" in that it actively exploits other people, may impoverish or kill them, and has the worst effect on the poorest people. It is obviously related to the very high unemployment rates. Also in this category would be the street gangs and terror networks.

A demographic winter?

In modern economic and political terms, what is not measured in a country is not valued, or even noticed. By revising our calculations of "economically active" and "dependent" people within a population we can provide a basis for much more realistic policies. Obviously - unlike age categories - the dividing lines between the different groups I am suggesting are uncertain: for example, someone may be unemployed but occasionally earn a bit of money. Definitions would have to be worked on, and perhaps arbitrary distinctions made. This exercise would be well worth it, however, because it would highlight the real contributors and dependants within a population as a whole, and provide the background for more realistic policies.

These would have to include a new focus on the numbers of babies being born, the welfare of women as well as men, the value of unpaid work, and the importance of health and welfare services in promoting fitness and reducing dependency. It leads onto an even bigger question of how we define gross domestic product (GDP) and even economic growth and development as a whole, because of the importance of non-cash contributions to the welfare of individuals and society which are largely made by women, but not adequately valued. An example would be a grandparent raising grandchildren without being paid and with no support: an important contributor to society and certainly not a dependant on it.

It is time to get over the moral panic about the prospect of fewer babies and more older people, which some have even called a "demographic winter". This panic is hugely overstated even for the richer countries which have had rapid increases in life expectancy. It is also based on unreliable forecasts: in some countries where the age of death has increased it is now static or even falling. With the Covid-19 pandemic causing large numbers of extra deaths especially among older people, it is clear that the world's population may face further challenges as new infectious diseases appear on the scene.

There are many other indications that our age span may fall if predictions are right about the increasing resistance of bacteria to life-saving antibiotics: when these became available in the mid-1940s they led to a rapid fall in life-threatening infections and an equally rapid rise in life expectancy. Growing wealth can also undermine health, with increased smoking and the effects of unhealthy fast-food diets and lack of exercise, overweight and a rapid increase in Type-2 diabetes. In the UK, for instance, three million people already have this and it is estimated that a third of the population are pre-diabetic.

Population maturity

The exaggerated warnings of a supposedly "ageing population" are now being applied to areas where there is little or no sign of increased life expectancy, especially in sub-Saharan Africa which has the lowest percentage of older people in the world, and Latin America where numbers are also low and, although growing, are doing so only very slowly. In reality, as Elizabeth Leahy Madsen has pointed out, the process of what she describes as "population maturity" is slow, and for most countries any significant extension of life expectancy remains on the distant horizon. She argues that there is plenty of time to rethink what it could mean when it really does happen, if it does. As in the wealthier countries, if life expectancy does rise this would also mean a longer expectancy of healthy life and this could mean a boost, and not a threat, to economic development and growth.

The "second demographic dividend" of higher investment arises from the financial contributions made by older people who have had a long working life. They may continue to earn their own money while many have accumulated personal and pension savings, money which is invested in the productive economy and provides large numbers of jobs for the younger generation.

While many richer countries are benefitting from this process, it does depend on there being enough money around - including welfare benefits - and health systems which can keep people productive. Without this, a country might have significant numbers of older people but be unable to keep them fit and healthy. The main examples here are Russia, which has high rates of chronic illness and disability, and the

United States, where many people cannot save enough to meet their needs in retirement, including medical treatment when they need it. In poor countries the relatively few people who do live into older age have generally not earned enough to save, and too often face real poverty. Traditionally they would have been supported by younger family members, but for some of them these support systems are breaking down. This seems to be a particular issue in China. The solutions lie in tackling the welfare problems to ensure self-reliance and health for older people, and care for those who need it.

Of course towards the end of their lives some older people in all countries do become dependent, and may eventually need help with their health and daily tasks. Governments in countries where this is a real issue need to come up with innovative schemes to match the "really old" with the increasing numbers of what has been called "young old" retired people, many of them on reasonable pensions, who have plenty of time and often many of the skills needed. Many of those retirees already provide many hours of voluntary work for friends, family and the community at large, while others complain of not having enough to do. Perhaps they could be offered a form of partnership or co-operative scheme where they enrol as informal carers for others, and in return get a guarantee that if they then need informal care later on it will be there for them.

Together with better help and support for full-time family carers, and a good back-up service for those with the most acute needs, especially in their own homes, the quality and effectiveness of care can be hugely improved compared to what is on offer at present. New Zealand is a leader in developing a comprehensive strategy for end-of-life and palliative care, based on advance care plans which are drawn up in consultation with patients, backed by sophisticated communication systems and specialist training for the health practitioners who work in geriatric care.

Dorian Gray RIP

A healthy population will have a balance of different ages, together with systems for supporting those who really need it: children, the unemployed, and people with severe illness or disabilities. As people become healthier and death rates at all ages decline, there will inevitably be more individuals living longer. This is a symptom of success, not failure. We all, as individuals, are getting older from the day we are born until the day we die, and to see this as some kind of disaster is a distortion of our human aspirations as well as our well-being as a society.

So let the demographers and politicians celebrate age as well as youth, seeing all of us as an essential resource. Can we finally ditch the fearful spectre of an "ageing society" and instead see increased life expectancy as our final rejection of premature death as a limiter of population? An increasing average age of the population is natural and inevitable as soon as fertility rates begin to fall. From an economic perspective, ageing that happens early in the demographic transition is a good thing because it signals that the age structure is becoming more balanced, the real dependency ratio is falling, and a larger percentage of the population is composed of working-age people who can generate income.

The "ageing" scare? Dorian Gray still lives, it seems. It is time to lay him quietly to rest.

Resources

"Does China have an ageing problem?", China Power website, June 2021.

Jack A Goldstone et al, eds, *Political Demography: How Population Changes are Reshaping International Security and National Politics* (Paradigm and Pluto Press, 2012)

David Kilcullen, *Out of the Mountains: The coming age of the urban guerrilla*, (Hurst, 2013)

Elizabeth Leahy Madsen, "For Fast-Growing Countries, Should Aging Be A Concern? Planning for the Second Demographic Dividend" The Wilson Centre website, 10 September 2013.

Jeroen Spijker and John MacInnes, "Population ageing: the timebomb that isn't?" *British Medical Journal,* 12 November 2013.

Chapter five

CATHOLIC MEN: OBSESSIONS AND INFALLIBILITY

"Though I speak with the tongues of men and of angels, and have not charity, I am become as sounding brass, or a tinkling cymbal."

"And though I have the gift of prophecy, and understand all mysteries, and all knowledge; and though I have all faith, so that I could remove mountains, and have no charity, I am nothing."

(First letter from St Paul to the Corinthians, 13: 1-2. *King James Bible*, Cambridge edition)

Does the Catholic hierarchy have the gift of charity? Many critics would say they put dogma first - seeking perhaps to remove mountains with it - while closing their ears to the needs of the people. In the western Catholic tradition they are all celibate males, they observe, constantly obsessed with women's bodies while ignorant of how women really live their lives. Even more important, perhaps, they have never had children (not legally, anyway) and do not live in families, so have no personal experience of what it really means to take care of children even though they preach long and loud about what "the family" should be (as if there is only one rigid model rather than the glorious variety that exists in reality).

One of my favourite stories is from Boccaccio's *Decameron*. Some Catholic priests were trying to convert a Jewish man to their religion and thought they were doing splendidly until he told them he was so impressed by their faith that he was going to make a pilgrimage to Rome. They were horrified: one look at the corruption and excesses of the Vatican at that time and their convert would run a mile. He returned, but full of enthusiasm and determined to be baptised. Why? He explained: if a Church is vibrant enough to thrive in the hearts of the people in spite of all that happens in Rome, it must indeed be close to God.

I am reminded of this story as I look at the Catholic hierarchy's campaign to promote Catholic births, and particularly its campaign to stop people using contraception and abortion. In the name of a "pro-life" mission, and contrary to the traditions of the Church in past ages, from the end of the 19th century they have made this their number one cause, the subject of endless decrees and dogmas, and sometimes with greater priority for their attention than the genuine life issues such as murder, capital punishment or wars. In the 1930 document *Casti Connubii* ("On Chaste Wedlock") the then Pope Pius XI declared artificial contraception to be "intrinsically evil," something that could never be permitted for any reason. Even murder is not considered by the Church to be in this category. The hierarchy have even, at times, traded a tolerance for extreme cruelty in a country in return for governments' adherence to their "Life" crusade. Catholic priests have been accused of justifying or even promoting torture and murder in Argentina and Rwanda, for example, in return for greater political commitment to their campaigns against family planning.

This obsession with stopping women from planning their pregnancies is all the more strange because virtually all the church's own members now ignore the hierarchy's teachings on family choice if contraceptives are available. In Spain and Italy, both of them strongly Catholic, birth rates have dropped dramatically to near-replacement levels. In the United States, the Guttmacher Institute reported in 2011 that 87% of Catholic women at risk of unplanned pregnancy were using contraceptives, barely below the national average of 88%. Among women of reproductive age who had ever had sex, 98% of Catholic women had used contraceptives compared to 99% of all women. So the number of Catholics obeying their Church's teachings against artificial contraception is minimal - as low as one in a hundred. It is likely that the findings would be similar in other countries provided there was easy access to family planning and the Church had not managed to prevent that through pressure on governments.

It has been suggested that the hierarchy's extreme vehemence on this issue is precisely because of their failure to enforce their teachings among their own members. What this means in practice is that in countries where they have overwhelming political power - including Ireland, the Philippines, and much of Latin America - they have been all the more determined to block people's access to contraceptive services, and especially legal and safe abortion, by putting relentless pressure on the governments to pass legislation or issue decrees. They can also use their monopoly provision of health services in many parts of the developing world to make sure that people cannot get contraception or safe abortions. For millions of the poorest people around the world, health provision is either a Catholic "mission" hospital or clinic, or nothing at all. Even for the wealthy elite, in many developing countries the main Catholic hospital is often the best (and most expensive) available to them. That will certainly not be offering family planning services or safe terminations, although wealthier people would have access to clinics elsewhere.

Why does the Catholic Church have such a powerful influence on the issue of choice about childbirth? It is partly its enormous membership in so many countries of the world. This is compounded by its near-monopoly on medical services in many of the poorest areas. Even more important, however, is the enormous amount of "diplomatic" and lobbying work undertaken at the United Nations, international conferences, and with many individual governments to block people's access to contraception and safe abortion, as we shall see in Chapter 7.

Babies left to die

For such a high-profile element of the Catholic Church's teachings and dogma, you might assume that this has been an article of faith either from Jesus's teachings or starting with the very early Church. This is not so.

The Catholic theologian Christine Gudorf has pointed out that Christianity evolved in a world in which contraception and abortion were known about, and widely used. Egyptians, Jews, Greeks and Romans are known to have used pessaries, potions and condoms made out of a wide variety of natural materials including animal skins, as well as coitus interruptus (the man withdrawing before ejaculation) while abortion also seems to have been widespread. Medieval Islamic physicians listed 196 contraceptive substances. Vaginal sponges and douches were often used. A Greek legend described a female condom made of a goat's bladder. The same was true of abortion: toxic herbs were widely used around the world. Two thousand years ago a wild fennel growing all around the Mediterranean area, which was used to terminate pregnancy, was used so extensively that it became extinct.

However the most important method of limiting family size was, sadly, infanticide - often recorded as "smothering" or "rolling over", or deaths recorded as "stillbirths" when in fact the babies died after birth. Unwanted babies were left unfed, deliberately killed, or abandoned with little or no food or clothing. Of the Church's response, Gudorf writes:

> *"The primary pastoral battles in the first millennium were around infanticide, the banning of which undoubtedly raised the incidence of abandonment."*

Abandonment meant babies left to die of hunger, thirst and cold, abandoned in wild areas to be killed by animal predators or left in the road for anybody to take. If these babies survived this would often mean lifelong slavery or abuse, living lives of great suffering and perhaps an early death. To ease the crisis and the human agony - of the mothers as well as the children - the Church in the Middle Ages encouraged people to offer babies they could not care for to foundling hospitals or to the Church, to be brought up as celibate nuns and monks who would serve the Church all their lives. Although they were denied a family life, either as children or adults, this was at least better than the alternative. It was also an important human resource for the Church itself.

The history of the Church's teachings on contraception and abortion up to the 19th century shows absolutely no consistency on these issues. No proclamations against it have been found in any biblical texts, and extensive research has failed to find them in the history of the early Church either. The first pontifical intervention found was in 1484 when Europe was starting to recover from the massive epidemic known as the Black Death, which had killed millions of people. Inquisitor Kramer urged Pope Innocent VIII to act against sorcerers who, he claimed,

> *"hinder men from performing the sexual act and women from conceiving."*

Despite these kinds of view the Church as a whole did not take any kind of position on contraception and abortion until the use of latex rubber led to improved and mass-produced condoms at the end of the 19th century. Perhaps as a hangover from older times the Church allows and even promotes supposedly "natural" birth control, otherwise known as the rhythm method, which calculates the recommended times for sex when the woman is least likely to be fertile. The main problem with it is that it can be quite stressful, requires a level of communication between couples that few can achieve, and does not work particularly well, although modern developments with computer and mobile phone apps have improved it. As the observer HL Mencken has written:

> *"It is now quite lawful for a Catholic woman to avoid pregnancy by resort to mathematics, though she is still forbidden to resort to physics or chemistry."*

Nobody could accuse the Church of a logical consistency.

Patron saints of abortion

Daniel Maguire, who has written extensively on the development of Church dogma on abortion in particular, has concluded that there was never a single teaching.

> *"The Roman Catholic position on abortion is pluralistic. It has a strong 'pro-choice' tradition and a conservative anti-choice tradition. Neither is official and neither is more Catholic than the other."*

Indeed, the present dogma depends not on any Catholic tradition but on resistance to a modern scientific understanding of pregnancy and childbirth. Until very recently, little was known about how embryos and foetuses developed before birth. It was even imagined that a man's sperm were little "homunculi" or miniature people (for this reason male masturbation was sometimes denounced as homicide). The equal role of the woman's eggs was not known and the development of the fertilised egg into a zygote, an embryo and then a foetus was also not understood. For this reason, at that time life or "ensoulment" was generally believed to start many weeks after conception, generally at the "quickening" when the woman could feel the foetus moving which was usually early in the fifth month of pregnancy. The woman was then viewed as the vessel for a future child which had developed fully formed out of the man's sperm.

The Church's traditional teachings about sex and childbirth were generally based on a view of women as intrinsically inferior, and a source of temptation that men should resist. It is an approach which even the most conservative man in the hierarchy would blush to acknowledge today although it may remain buried deep in their collective subconscious. As Daniel Maguire points out:

"A culture that looks on women as sources of evil like Pandora and Eve is going to have trouble justifying [men] having sex with them."

St Augustine wrote that were it not for reproduction, there would be no use for women at all. Some other early Church writers argued that women were like animals in that we lack reason, and only possess the image of God through connection to men. The feminist theologian Christine Gudorf points out that the Church has rejected this nonsense about women but:

"continues to teach most of the sexual moral code which was founded upon such thinking".

On the question of abortion, little was said specifically by the Church authorities until the 15th century, and even then many theologians justified it in particular cases which included the life and welfare of the mother. There is even a Catholic saint, a Florentine archbishop of the 15th century called St Antoninus, who argued that early abortions could not be considered murder because the foetus was not yet human. Influential writers of the 16th century and later went on to develop this view. The saint's namesake Antoninus of Corduba wrote that the health as well as the life of the mother were more important than continuing a risky pregnancy. Perhaps we should nominate the two St

Antoninuses as the official patron saints of World Population Day.

Even now, there are many different views among Catholic theologians and scholars on whether abortion is permissible in cases where there is danger of death for the mother, if conception occurred through rape, or if the foetus has died in the womb or is known to have a life-threatening disability. They would be well aware that Catholic families - like all families - depend on the mother's key role if they are to thrive, and therefore Catholic children need their mother to survive. You would not think that these alternative views existed within the Church, however, if you listen only to the hierarchy in Rome.

A recent scandal in Ireland highlights the extreme bias in parts of the Catholic Church towards promoting births without concern for the welfare of the babies. A mass grave of babies and children was discovered, some of them in a septic tank, at the former Bon Secours children's home in Tuam, Galway in 2017. They had been taken from unmarried mothers in an atmosphere of "shame" over many decades which made it almost impossible for the women to keep their children. Ireland became known as an easy place to adopt babies with few checks on the families and some were sold, often to American families who had not been vetted as suitable parents, or even to men on their own who lied that they had a wife.

Some of the babies in Tuam had been allowed to die in childbirth or in infancy and either buried without proper records or simply discarded in the tank where there was human waste. Some babies, born with a disability, were left to starve to death. Meanwhile many of the women were made to work without pay in Church-run laundries, continually told that they were wicked and sinful. No attempt was made by the Church to locate and work with the fathers, or to call them sinful for having sex outside marriage: the old double standard between women and men was rigorously upheld. Although the Bon Secours and similar homes have now been closed, it is estimated that 6,000 babies died in similar Church-run homes throughout Ireland.

A very similar scandal over church-run children's homes arose in Canada in 2021. The Canadian Government had been forcibly separating native American children from their parents and putting them into religious-run homes, to "assimilate" them or, as indigenous people have said, as part of a "cultural genocide". A mass grave was found at the Catholic-run Kamloops Indian Residential School, which had been open since 1890 and only handed over to the Government in 1969. The horrors of what in effect was stealing children from their indigenous families went almost up to the present day: the policy was only discontinued in 1998. Its features in relation to children are quite similar to what western countries now accuse the Chinese about in the case of the Uighur people there, and also strikingly similar to the Nazi policies of the "Lebensborn", complete with children gathering to gaze out of the windows in the hope that their parents would come to get them.

"Rome has locked the door"

The Catholic hierarchy's implacable - one might even say obsessive - opposition to contraception and abortion started as late as the end of the 19th century, when some modern methods were just beginning to become available. This opposition was reinforced in the 20th century, probably as a reaction to the continuing improvements in those methods, as well as the easier access to them for women and couples who wanted to plan their families.

The dogma is closely tied up with the notion of authority in the Church - exclusively male of course - and especially with the quite recent idea that the Pope, as head of the Church, was "infallible":

> *"In every instance where the pope intervenes the bishops are obliged to obey and submit to his decisions."*

It was a radical reversal of centuries of Catholic Church history.

A Pope's "direct sovereignty over the entire Church" dates back to 1870 when Pius IX was faced with the conquest of the Papal States by the nationalist forces fighting for a unified Italy. He was also facing a big expansion of the competing Protestant churches, as well as the secular revolutionary spirit epitomised by the French Revolution and 19th century popular movements for democracy and nationalism in Europe and worldwide.

With defeat on the battlefield by Garibaldi's unifying forces, Pius IX lost the historic secular powers which the Vatican had possessed to enforce authority in its own States through the arrest, imprisonment and even execution of opponents. It is telling perhaps that the last execution of a citizen of the Papal States took place just six weeks before the formal introduction of the dogma of papal infallibility. It has been suggested that Pius was seeking a new absolute power over spiritual and doctrinal matters in the Church as a substitute for the lost power of life and death over his citizens. He was also under intense criticism from the popular press and from opinion within the Church.

"God on earth"?

At the time, this new dogma of papal infallibility was strongly opposed by many in the Church. Many bishops felt that Pius IX was insincere, malicious, perhaps insane, and using lies and trickery to force through a decision in his favour. One diarist wrote at the time:

> "Oh, this unfortunate pope. How much evil he has done!"

The Catholic historian Franz Xavier Kraus wrote in his diary in 1900:

> "Rome has locked the door leading to its only way out. There seems to be nothing left but for the whole papal system to break down."

He was wrong. Although the doctrine of infallibility was controversial it was accepted by Church members as a whole, probably because it chimed with their own needs in a world full of turmoil. Mumford argues:

> "Infallibility provides many believers with a great sense of religious security all through life, imparting stability and freedom from anxiety, relieving emotional pressure and softening the cruel blows of reality."

In other words their personal welfare and happiness, both in this world and the next, depend on obedience to the Pope. He alone could provide a guarantee of their own salvation after death. The well-connected Catholic writer John Bosco, who did much to promote the new doctrine of infallibility, even referred to the Pope as "God on earth". Pius IX has now been beatified by subsequent Popes, followed later by Bosco.

On the subject of contraception and abortion, major pronouncements were made in 1930 (with the encyclical *Casti connubii*), in 1951 (Pius X11's *Address to Midwives*), and 1958 (*Address to the Society of Haemotology*). Finally in 1968 came the encyclical *Humanae Vitae* ("On Human Life") in which Pope Paul VI condemned practically every form of birth control as morally reprehensible. The Encyclical outlaws completely:

> *"any action which either before, at the moment of, or after sexual intercourse, is specifically intended to prevent procreation".*

A fragile dogma

The sequence of events here shows just how fragile the dogma is. It could easily have gone in the opposite direction, if only Pope John XXIII had lived a little longer. He is thought to have taken that name, incidentally, after the 14th-century Pope John XXII who had condemned claims of his own "infallibility" as the work of the devil. When John XXIII set up his Papal Commission on Population and Birth in 1963, in response to the development of the contraceptive pill, it was a signal that the Church could change its position on birth planning in spite of the infallibility and authority principles. The Commission included leading Catholic theologians together with bishops and doctors, and even included five women.

In 1966 it reported, with strong majorities recommending change, that artificial birth control was not intrinsically evil and that Catholic couples should be allowed to decide for themselves about the methods to be employed. According to this report, use of contraceptives should be regarded as an extension of the already accepted rhythm or cycle method. Unfortunately John XXIII had already died by the time the report was published. A minority report was dominated by the Polish cardinal Wojtyla (later Pope John Paul II) who insisted that any change of doctrine would be giving in to "the Protestants" and would mean conceding that the Holy Spirit had indeed been on the Protestant side. The new Pope Paul VI accepted this argument and turned the clock right back, using the minority report as justification, and issued *Humanae Vitae*.

Paul VI accepted Wojtyla's argument that changing the dogma on contraception would undermine the authority of previous Church teachings. In effect the hierarchy is insisting on opposing contraception and abortion just because they have done so previously, even if that was wrong. Wojtyla wrote:

> *"If it should be declared that contraception is not evil in itself, then we should have to concede frankly that the Holy Spirit had been on the side of the Protestant Churches… This would mean that the leaders of the Church, acting with extreme imprudence, had condemned thousands of innocent human acts, forbidding, under pain of eternal damnation, a practice which would now be sanctioned…"*

Pope Paul VI followed his adoption of the minority report with a sweeping purge of the many leading Church officials and theologians who had backed the majority report. The bishops of fourteen different countries had respectfully disagreed with the new dogma, and told their own Church members they could follow their own consciences. In many cases it was to cost them their jobs and career prospects, and the Church lost some outstanding leaders.

If all this seems like the reaction of a dictator to any real or imagined threats to their authority, it reflects badly on a Church supposedly open to forgiveness and charity. Although the notion of papal infallibility is rarely used in a formal "ex cathedra" sense, it creates an aura of unquestionable authority on all decisions and announcements by successive Popes, even if they are different from their predecessors'. What is extraordinary is that among all the moral challenges in the modern world it is the issue of women, and our ability to decide on childbearing, which is seen by the authorities as the key test of the Pope's infallibility, and indeed of the Church's overall authority.

"The real treasures of wisdom"

The Catholic Church, over the centuries, has shown that it can adjust to changing times, a changing economy, and new science, even though this is sometimes slow and reluctant. It no longer persecutes scientists such as Galileo, or forbids the payment of interest on loans, for example - previously seen as evil and strictly forbidden. The most notable recent example of major change is on the sexual abuse of children by priests, where the Church has turned from denial to condemnation although only after a long and very painful battle by abuse victims and their supporters. The Church's official view of women has yet to be tackled: advocates of women's rights and needs are vocal within as well as outside the Church but they are nowhere near strong enough to force a change of heart at the top.

Perhaps an all-male priesthood is just deeply resistant to women. The retired Pope Benedict XVI, when he was a

Vatican official, had even raised the spectre of the old fear of women, drafting an attack on the women's movement which was issued as *A Letter to the Bishops of the Catholic Church on the Collaboration of Men and Women*. This claimed that feminist thought had destroyed "the family" and that it had induced women to see themselves as "the adversaries of men". As the philosopher Diana Maffia commented, the Letter fails to understand the women's movement but is a knee-jerk reaction to it:

> *"It is not an invitation to dialogue, it attempts to enforce silence, undermine authority and make veiled threats."*

Maguire sees this kind of thinking as a distortion of the Church's true message. He suggests that power in the Church is separated from ideas, which is a matter of real tragedy.

> *"The Catholic tradition is more filled with good sense and flexibility than one would gather from its leaders"*

but popes and bishops, appointed by the existing hierarchy, are often bureaucratic careerists or natural conservatives who:

> *"often do not express the real treasures of wisdom that Catholicism has to offer to the world."*

Is it possible that this wisdom could in the end prevail over the hierarchy in the matter of choice about having children? The purged Catholic theologian Hans Kung has concluded:

> *"The only way to solve the problem of contraception is to solve the problem of infallibility."*

But there are Catholics who see the possibility of change based on a new focus on charity rather than authority, with a willingness to listen, especially to the poor, as preached by the current Pope, Francis. This remains to be seen. Francis is hated by many conservatives within the Catholic Church and one prominent English priest even told the London *Guardian*:

> *"We can't wait for him to die. Whenever two of us meet, we talk about how awful he is."*

The atmosphere is poisonous, with Pope Francis telling the Italian newspaper *La Repubblica:*

> *"Heads of the church have often been narcissists, flattered and thrilled by their courtiers. The court is the leprosy of the papacy."*

There are entrenched attitudes and careers lined up behind the idea of papal authority, rather than the actual person of the Pope, and they have chosen the ban on modern family planning as their litmus test for loyalty. The Vatican's diplomatic missions around the world, especially at the United Nations, have for many years been devoted to undermining or blocking proposals to help women make our own decisions on sex and pregnancy. Bishops and cardinals in many countries have devoted massive efforts to lobbying governments to block choice. It is hard to see this edifice of opposition being dismantled any time soon. The most we might hope for is a reduction and softening of the campaign, and a redirection of some of the funding towards more charitable activities.

Witch hunts and a new Inquisition

I suggest that the "Life" dogma, and the ferocious battles against contraception and abortion, are comparable to the medieval Inquisitions. The Catholic Church, alongside all the good it has done, has a shameful history of pursuing unbelievers, Protestants, "heretics", scientists and dissidents, real or imagined. They included at one time their own Church members in majority Catholic countries who had been forced to convert from Islam and Judaism, but were regarded as unreliable - prime targets for interrogation methods that would often lead to forced "confessions". With the book *Malleus Maleficarum* ("The Hammer of Witches"), elements of the Church also prompted and encouraged the medieval craze for witch-hunting, aimed mainly at women, although it was never official Church policy. Two of the questions in this text were:

> *"Whether Witches can Hebetate [prevent] the Powers of Generation."*
>
> *"That Witches who are Midwives in Various Ways Kill the Child Conceived in the Womb, and Procure an Abortion; or if they do not this Offer New-born Children to Devils."*

There have been many different Inquisitions within the Catholic Church over the centuries, starting in the 12th century and continuing in some areas until the mid-19th century. The best known to us was in Spain, but in fact they covered many European countries and were vigorously pursued in the Spanish and Portuguese colonies in Latin America, Africa and Asia. Suspects who were accused of "heretical" beliefs, or not conforming in some way, were tortured by priests, monks and others. Those convicted were handed over to civil authorities for imprisonment, banishment and execution, often by being burned alive. It was a campaign of terror: in fact a 1578 handbook for inquisitors stated the objective as being:

> *"in order that others may become terrified and weaned away from the evils they would commit".*

After the Reformation, with some European countries becoming officially Protestant, the Church conducted violent campaigns to force people back into the fold, in what was known as the Counter-Reformation. This involved not only individual persecution but also war (the French religious wars and the Thirty Years War) and massacres such as the St Bartholomew's Day Massacre in 1572 with a wave of Catholic mob violence against Protestants in Paris and other French cities. All this, sadly, was in the name of their Church's unquestionable authority, justifying the use of terror with charity nowhere to be seen.

With the Catholic hierarchy's modern Inquisition the main targets are now the women who will not or cannot conform to their authority, whether inside or outside the Church itself. There is obviously no physical torture done by priests themselves, and thankfully no murder. However the result is the same: the suffering and death of women and their children, enforced through the secular authorities by means of laws which the Church has demanded. Women are being exposed to the pain, disability and death which can result from too many pregnancies, the enormous risks of childbirth without good hygiene and medical care, and especially from illegal and botched abortions which are the result of desperate attempts to end unwanted pregnancies. Far too many of the babies born are also condemned to hunger and poverty, sometimes disability and an early death - especially if their mothers die, but also if there are more children than the family can support.

The inquisitorial approach also fosters and encourages verbal aggression, harassment and threats against women using family planning clinics, as well as the murder of doctors, arson, bomb attacks and sabotage of the clinics themselves. We will explore this further in Part Three. Some of those involved in this harassment are Catholics, others are not, but all are encouraged and supported by Catholic "Life" dogma and generous support and funding from the Church. A priest called Father Paul Marx, who claims "contraception-sterilisation-abortion" is a "worldwide plague," has set up Human Life International, whose spokesman Don Treshman praised the sniper shooting of a member of clinic staff in Canada as a "superb tactic". He also started a fund for the convicted killer of a doctor in the US. No action has been taken against these people by the hierarchy.

Where, you wonder, is the Vatican's "pro-life" condemnation of criminal attacks on clinics and their staff, including murder, or those who seek to justify or cover up these attacks? If the hierarchy are not directly responsible for the propaganda, violence and intimidation, why do they not issue guidelines for appropriate behaviour by protesters outside clinics?

Where is the acknowledgement of the suffering and deaths of so many women who are forced to carry a pregnancy that will not produce a healthy baby, or where they cannot deliver safely? How do they weigh up the effect of their own bans on contraception, and the desperate abortions that result? Where is the understanding that many children are born only to suffer and die because of this? And where is the care for the women, the understanding of their needs, or support for those who help them? To an outsider, as for many good Catholics, it makes no sense at all: plenty of removing mountains but strictly no charity.

Some have argued that this is all a reaction to what Church members are actually doing. The less their members obey their dogmas, the more the authorities are determined to use their political influence to block contraception and abortion so that it is put out of reach to everybody, Catholic or not. The campaign by the hierarchy is unrelenting. Under the banner of Life, theirs is a fight to the death.

"How can an increase in births be promoted?"

A flurry of excitement greeted moves by Pope Francis, at his inauguration, to re-emphasise the need to listen to the poor. However, although he is less judgmental about individual "sins" he shows little or no understanding of the lives of poor women, or the decisions they face throughout their lives. Observers within the Church have concluded that he is personally opposed to contraception. Indeed, he recently instructed married couples to "be fruitful and multiply," and criticised them for spending time looking after cats and dogs when they could be having children. He also claimed that if a couple remained childless they would ultimately have nothing but "the bitterness of loneliness". It is a surprising threat, coming from a man who is a lifelong celibate with no family and certainly no children. Is the celibate priestly life then so unbearable?

A Vatican survey issued in November 2013, under Pope Francis, asked how people were receiving the Church's messages on family matters, ahead of a Family Synod in 2014 which would put particular emphasis on homosexuality and sexual relationships outside marriage. The question on contraception, though, was:

> *"How can a more open attitude towards having children be fostered? How can an increase in births be promoted?"*

Again it is the focus on numbers and not individuals, with no reference to the health of the mother or the welfare of children and families. If even more births are the answer, what is the question? Perhaps it is: how can we force women to have more children against their will?

So although the hierarchy can change, or at least think about changing its attitude to gay people and relationships, or the abuse of children by priests - or even appointing a few women to positions in the Church - it shows no sign of rethinking its commitment to maximising births.

Perhaps the most one can expect from the current Catholic hierarchy is to reduce the vast amounts of Church funds which go into the campaigns against international or national programmes for women's choice. They could issue a call to "pro-lifers" to stop harassing women, threatening the clinics, justifying arson and murder, and pushing a deliberately false story about pregnancy and birth. For the rest, it would require Francis and the bishops to do a different kind of "listening to the poor" which would mean listening to poor women in order to understand who they are, how they live, and why they make the decisions they do. One recent statement by Pope Francis allowed priests to "forgive" women for abortions. However, the language used was that of right-wing abortion opponents in the United States:

> *"The tragedy of abortion is experienced by some with a superficial awareness, as if not realizing the extreme harm that such an act entails. Many others, on the other hand, although experiencing this moment as a defeat, believe that they have no other option. I think in particular of all the women who have resorted to abortion."*

This is the assumption that women are "victims" because they cannot make informed decisions about their own lives. It perhaps speaks loudly of Francis's alignment with a particular kind of conservative male view, rather than an ability to listen to the millions of women who have to make their own choices.

Those liberal Catholic commentators who hope for a more substantive relaxation of the official position on this emphasise the role in Church teachings of the "*sensus fidelium*", the common sense of the faithful Church members based on their own experience and conscience. The Spanish have a saying:

"An ounce of mother is worth more than a pound of clergy."

They cite the example of how this has worked in the case of the centuries-old ban on the "sin of usury" - charging interest on loans. This teaching was quietly dropped as Church members persisted in borrowing and lending with interest. In fact the Church now has its own bank which commits usury all day, every day. So much for a supposed "sin", conveniently forgotten when the notion becomes ridiculous. Or as an English saying has it: if you can't beat them, join them.

Gudorf comments that with most Church members using contraception if they can, and abortion when necessary, in the future the hierarchy could come to recognise that their members are right and that the biosphere is threatened by the sheer number of its teeming human inhabitants. They could, she suggests, "discern the will of God and the presence of the Spirit" in the choices of those who:

"share responsibility for the lives and health and prosperity of future generations"

by having few children, or none.

It is interesting that many Catholic nuns understand the issues far better than the hierarchy. Nuns in the US, who work mainly with the most disadvantaged people, have united to issue a statement justifying contraception. There are reports of subversion among nuns in Catholic hospitals: a friend told me she knew someone in hospital in Germany, for treatment after a botched abortion, who was talking to a nun in the next bed. The nun whispered to her:

> *"Why don't you use the 'Mary Magdalen' technique? All the prostitutes use it."*

This was cotton wool coated with oil. It is perhaps not the most sophisticated method, and quite old-fashioned, but certainly better than nothing. And the nuns working with the poorest women understand their need.

"Enormous good and enormous evil"

Others are much more pessimistic about any real change at the top. Catholics for Choice observes:

> *"The Catholic hierarchy has its own politics. In a world where power is sought after and ordained for the long term, taking a reactionary stance on controversial issues can be rewarding - the old guard gets to preserve the status quo, while newcomers rise faster when not making waves. On a deeper level, however, the all-male, celibate hierarchy can avoid any honest confrontation about sexuality by insisting that sex is simply a function of procreation."*

The hierarchy is still deaf to the needs of the people. I am reminded of the Bible's saying from Jesus:

> *"Or what man is there of you, whom if his son ask bread, will he give him a stone?"* (Matthew, 7:9)

In an open letter of 2008, fifty pro-choice Catholic organisations in different countries wrote that the ban on contraception:

> *"has had catastrophic effects on the poor and weak of the whole world, putting in danger the lives of women and exposing millions of people to the risk of contracting HIV."*

There has been no response from Rome.

Frances Kissling, President of Catholics for a Free Choice, was asked whether the Church had been mostly a force for good or a force for ill. She replied:

> *"There are certainly days when I believe that the institution is so deeply corrupted that it should be destroyed. I think of all the ways in which people who have been part of this Church have been abused: priests who want to get married, women who want to be priests, women who use contraception, gay people. At the same time, some of the very same people who can be so abusive to their family have done great social good: Catholic education, Catholic health care. There are parts of the world where the only place you will be medically treated is by a Catholic. It does enormous good and enormous evil."*

Resources

Professor Daniel C Maguire, "The Moderate Roman Catholic Position on Contraception and Abortion" Marquette University (available on the internet)

Frederic Ballenegger, "The Ethics and Theology of Population Dynamics," unpublished paper, 12 December 2012.

Christine Gudorf, *Body, Sex and Pleasure: Reconstructing Christian Sexual Ethics* (Pilgrim Press, 1995)

"Letter to the Bishops of the Catholic Church on the Collaboration of Men and Women in the Church and in the World", 2004, signed by Cardinal Joseph Ratzinger [now the retired Pope Benedict XVI] and Angelo Amato, and approved by Pope John Paul II.

Andrew Brown, "The War against Pope Francis," The Guardian, London, 28 October 2017.

Stephen D Mumford, *The Life and Death of NSSM 200: How the Destruction of Political Will Doomed a US Population Policy* (Amazon.com, 1996).

PART THREE

BATTLES

Chapter six

PRO-LIFERS ATTACK, WOMEN RETREAT

Everyone - especially every woman - needs to be able to decide whether to have children, and when would be the best time. It is essential for our own health and welfare, for good sexual and family relationships, and to support ourselves, our families and our communities. This underpins equal rights in society and the workplace, freeing women from unwanted pregnancies and the struggle to maintain all those children who were never planned. Modern contraception is also essential to stabilise our population numbers. It is not so long ago that Europe was exporting large numbers of its people to colonies all around the world, with all the enduring conflict that still continues from that process. Now it is the poorest countries that have the highest rates of human population growth. Stabilising our numbers is essential if we are to preserve our whole environment, not just for our own benefit but as a legacy to future generations.

So why - when richer women can now have contraception and poorer women do not - is there such a guilty silence in the media and in international circles about the issue? Some of the organisations which should be discussing it have made it a taboo subject. This is in spite of the fact that there have been massive advances in the contraceptive methods available, and improvements in service delivery to meet people's needs effectively and safely, in even the poorest areas of the world. But this information is regarded as something not for discussion in polite society - an old-fashioned approach to sex and contraception that seems bizarre in our highly sexualised, porn-filled world. The knowledge of these advances seems to be confined to those working directly in sexual health services and is being ignored by many women's and environmental groups, as well as too many governments and international agencies which are supposedly working to eradicate poverty.

All too often we hear the defensive line about this being about supposed "population control". In fact nobody on the international scene is advocating this: it was discarded as a concept in the 1960s and 70s, since it seemed to suggest that "we" should control "them", the exact opposite of allowing everyone to make their own decisions. The single exception was the Chinese Government and its forced "one child" policy, and even this has now finally been relaxed to three children. They are now applying "population control" to the minority Uighurs, including forced sterilisations and abortions. We can hardly blame the family planning movement for the policies of the Chinese Government.

The real reason for the international reluctance to discuss the issues, I suggest, is the avoidance by many who have failed to connect with the reality of family planning methods and programmes. Many people are also keeping quiet because of the obsession of "pro-lifers" with abortion, an obsession which too often leads to aggression and the silencing of opponents. Behind the rhetoric about abortion, I suggest, lies a pro-natalist opposition also to contraception although this is rarely mentioned by them. The "pro-life" movement is made up of individuals, organisations, right-wing governments and some major religious forces like the Catholic Church and, increasingly, other fundamentalist Christian, Muslim and other groups. They are the real controlling force in this debate, they have enormous amounts of money, and they are highly organised.

Like all reactionary movements, it starts with propaganda: untruths endlessly repeated, together with the repetitive use of language which distorts reality. With the opposition to contraception and abortion it starts with endless repetition of myths about "unborn babies," "unborn children" or the "pre-born". This is a denial of the crucial importance of birth as the start of a life, and a contradiction to how all human societies view the start of a baby's life, in law and in the real world. It is birth that transforms a foetus into a baby. An "unborn baby," although it is a commonly used expression, is a contradiction in terms.

When a child is born

All human cultures celebrate birth. They aim to support the health and wellbeing of women who are pregnant so that at the end they can finally give birth to a child that will survive into adulthood. Our lives as humans start with our birth: this is the common-sense view, and always has been. People worldwide have always celebrated the birth of a baby as a momentous event: a new member of a family, community and society: a tiny new human being that we can see, touch and celebrate. A child can be part of the family and community only once she or he has been born.

The opposition work hard to give the impression that a fully formed tiny baby is living in the womb almost from the moment of conception and merely "growing" in preparation for birth. Pope Francis, among many others, has spoken of "an innocent child growing in the mother's womb". They use cleverly angled scans of foetuses, showing fingers but not the undeveloped internal organs, blown up to the size of a fully developed baby and not the tiny embryo or undeveloped foetus it really is. For these ideologues, birth is irrelevant and makes no real difference to the "pre-born" or "unborn baby". Therefore, they argue, even from the moment of conception the supposed "unborn baby" or "the preborn" is a fully developed human being. They argue that its rights are therefore the same as, or even greater than the people who are already living their own independent lives - especially the woman who is carrying the foetus and giving it life as part of her own body. Their case is based on a kind of propaganda that falsifies pictures, distorts language and is highly selective and dishonest in its use of scans and other modern medical techniques.

We now know that at conception, where the sperm fertilises the egg, it becomes a single-celled organism called a zygote. Over the next two weeks there is a germinal period, during which each cell divides into two to create a multi-celled organism called a blastocyst that then moves down the fallopian tube and has to implant into the woman's womb in order to develop further. This may develop to form one individual or two identical twins (and occasionally triplets). Implantation occurs when the cells nestle into the uterine lining and rupture tiny blood vessels. The connective web of blood vessels and membranes that form between them will provide nourishment for the developing being for the next nine months. There are many failures of implantation but if it succeeds the next stage is a tiny unformed embryo which then finally develops into a foetus. This gradually develops the nervous system and brain, sex organs, vital organs like liver, kidneys and heart, and the physical shape that will be necessary for independent life. At the end of the whole nine-month process, once the foetus has grown large enough and the lungs are finally developed, it will be ready to be born as a baby.

Until the mother gives birth to the foetus she has been carrying, whether conventionally or through surgery, it is on life support from her. This means it is entirely dependent on her existence, her breathing, her nutrition, her internal organs, her blood, and her health and wellbeing. If she thrives, it has the best possible chance of thriving also. If she starves, the foetus starves. If she dies (unless it can be delivered urgently by caesarean section) it will die with her. In a very real sense, the unborn foetus belongs to the mother since its body is a part of hers.

A new life

Modern medical research and practice has shown what a momentous event the birth of a baby is. At birth newborns become independent human beings, living and breathing on their own. They are expelled from the birth canal with liquid in their lungs: the sudden change to temperature and environment triggers a reaction in the central nervous system which prompts them to take their first breath within about ten seconds after birth. This expands their lungs and dramatically lowers the blood pressure in parts of their heart and other organs, switching their intake of oxygen and changing the circulation of blood - a process which takes about three minutes. They will then have an entirely new cardiovascular system which will be the basis of their whole life. Their nutrition will no longer be derived from their mothers through the placenta, but must be obtained independently whether from the mother's milk or other foods. All their organs, especially the liver, heart and lungs, must now start operating independently, or not at all.

Through modern medical procedures of life support involving the latest (and most expensive) technology, we have been able to push back the date at which a baby can be born prematurely, without fully developed organs, but still survive. We may have reached the limits of what is possible for premature births: it is considered unlikely that we can reduce these techniques to even lower ages of gestation.

Even the Catholic Church, now so vehement about "unborn babies", has always dated a baby's life from the moment of their birth. They have even refused, until very recently, to allow baptism for miscarried foetuses or babies who die in the womb or during the birth. For centuries, when child mortality was extremely high, the churches even used to delay baptism of a baby until it was certain that she or he would survive the first few days and be able to live into the future. That basic logic about the start of life is now being challenged by the "pro-lifers" with a very ancient idea, arising from ignorance of human reproduction, that women were merely containers or "vessels" for a man's sperm, contributing nothing of their own to the future baby. There are strong overtones of the "vessel" image in much of what the Catholic Church and many fundamentalists are saying on this subject now: that the "unborn" are more important than the women who carry and nurture them, and give them life.

Women as deserters?

Seen as vessels or containers, women can be treated almost as equipment for the production of babies, and even as appendages to their own "unborn" - without dignity and without choice. Even if a woman's health or even her life are threatened by the pregnancy, she must then be forced to continue it even against her will. If she is married but has no children, she should be "encouraged" to join the motherhood club. Hence the increasingly adamant dogma against modern contraception by the Catholic Church, and its ferocious opposition to termination once pregnancy is even suspected. It sometimes appears as if the men in the hierarchy are seeing any pregnancy as "ours", to be protected at all costs, unlike the women who are "other" and of less importance. It enables a focus on numbers rather than genuine nurture, and on babies as property.

This is the subject of vicious battles in the United States which are reaching levels of absurdity which extends to arguments about taxes. In November 2017 Republicans in the House of Representatives passed extremist foetal "personhood" language as part of a tax bill. The US Senate were considering a separate plan that similarly considers an "unborn child…at any stage of development" (from the moment of conception as a fertilised egg) as a tax beneficiary, in a move that takes the campaign against women's reproductive rights to the level of wanting to give them National Insurance numbers. Is this a new version of "Invasion of the Body-snatchers", only with women's bodies the subject of invasion?

This was certainly the view of the Romanian dictator Nicolae Ceausescu who ordered the criminal investigation of any miscarriages. He outlawed contraception as well as abortion, and subjected girls and women to invasive monthly gynaecological examinations to identify and monitor any pregnancies.

> *"The foetus is the socialist property of the whole society. Giving birth is a patriotic duty… Those who refuse to have children are deserters."*

The result was the highest rate of maternal deaths in Europe, and huge numbers of orphans and abandoned children whose families could not care for them. There was also a wave of secret and very dangerous abortions.

The notion of women as containers or carriers for "unborn children" has become a staple of right-wing masculinist movements, which are often fiercely opposed to women's equality and independence. Racist ideas of eugenics - increasing "our" numbers in a battle with "the other" - are often put forwards by fascist organisations. In Italy, for example, right-wing skinheads are reported to have attended a rally where they used the fascist salute of one outstretched arm, some of them wearing a "9%" badge - a classic eugenic reference to the percentage of the world population that they categorise as "white".

A climate of aggression and fear in Italy is having an effect on medical services: seven out of ten doctors there now say they would refuse to carry out terminations of pregnancy, whatever the risks of that pregnancy or the needs of the woman concerned. The refusals have been rising, from 59% in 2005 to 70% in 2013, and have led to a predictable increase in the number of desperate women self-administering or having illegal abortions. One woman who was admitted to an Italian hospital for termination of a pregnancy, where the foetus had no chance of surviving beyond birth, was forced to wait for several days in induced labour for the one doctor who would help her to come on shift. Since there has been no rise in religious affiliation in Italy (quite the opposite) and no indication that doctors are becoming more religious, it appears that the doctors are increasingly worried about their career prospects and even their safety in the face of increasingly aggressive "pro-lifers".

"We will kill"

Battles over control of women and the "unborn" are going on in almost every part of the world. However, the country where this fight has become most bitter is the United States, where right-wing Christian fundamentalists and evangelicals have joined the Catholic bishops in their campaign. Michelle Goldberg has suggested that this move represents a fierce backlash against rapid social change in general, and the women's movement in particular:

"As a synecdoche [representation] *for American social chaos, abortion was a powerful political motivator."*

Although contraception and abortion are legal in the US,

clinics which provide these services find themselves under sustained misrepresentation and attack. Death threats from the "pro-lifers" are daily occurrences. Some of the more violent activists have murdered doctors and clinic staff by means of arson, bombings and shooting - using the tactics of terrorism, in fact. Between 1977 and mid-2016 there were 11 murders, 26 attempted murders, 42 bombings, 185 cases of arson, and thousands more incidents of criminal behaviour including threats, personal smears, harassment and intimidation. They include publicising the personal details and addresses of clinic staff and even on their children, leading to threats of violence or even murder against them.

The attacks have been escalating, especially after the release of propaganda videos in 2015 deliberately falsified to claim that clinics "murder children" and sell "baby parts". A security firm identified more than 25,000 incidents of online threats to clinics and staff in just six weeks. One anonymous caller to a hospital switchboard said:

"We will kill all abortion doctors."

Another threatened to set all the clinics on fire. The threats are alarming credible since all this has indeed happened. They inspire great fear and have indeed driven many doctors and health staff out of the work. One family planning doctor found her name, personal and professional details and photos of herself and her child on an anti-choice website which claimed she was part of an "abortion cartel".

> *"There is no better way to intimidate and incite fear than to target a family member, especially a child. The message is unambiguous: I'm being watched, and so is my daughter."*

Intimidation extends also to the media. A children's author, Judy Blume, who has spoken out in defence of the Planned

Parenthood organisation, had over 700 hate-mail warnings:

> *"We know where you are going to be and we'll be there waiting for you."*

Planned Parenthood's Fred Clarkson researched the anti-abortion militias in the United States and was invited onto a major TV network to speak about it. This was cancelled at short notice:

> *"because they'd have angry pro-life viewers calling in and they didn't want to take that heat".*

Battles

The FBI and local police have been trying to stop all this and have been involved in protecting clinics and breaking up groups of people who were blockading the entrances. So far they have had little control of the situation. Attempts to prosecute the people creating the worst video have come to nothing. Many family planning services have been forced to spend a fortune on security and even struggle to maintain their buildings because local service providers have been put under pressure not to work for them. Some have even had to close clinics, especially in the poorest areas of the country and those serving the women of black and minority groups who have the least chance of travelling somewhere else for help.

The battles are also raging in State legislatures and in the courts. Former President Trump, who publicly backed pro-lifers on many occasions, packed both higher and lower courts with his own conservative nominees, a legacy that is long outlasting his departure from office. The pro-choice side is constantly being forced into legal fight to preserve what they have. One landmark decision in June 2016 saw the US

Supreme Court striking down extreme restrictions on access to abortion by the State of Texas - but there will be many more such attempts, and with the appointment of many conservative judges the decisions are more likely to go the other way in future, even in the Supreme Court which itself became very unbalanced in the direction of conservatives following the death of Ruth Bader Ginsburg. For women in the United States, despite the relief of finally defeating Trump in the 2020 presidential election, this is still a difficult time, having to fight yet again to safeguard what they had previously fought for and won.

Hard-line anti-abortionists have been found to be connected to far-right movements seeking power in the US and taking hundreds of millions of dollars in "dark money" from anonymous conservative donors. One investigator has discovered far-right activists justifying violence by claiming they should:

"take up arms and defend ourselves against the laws of man," with a "Doctrine of the Lesser Magistrate" to justify criminality. Twenty of the leading anti-abortionists were identified as taking part in the 2021 invasion of the US Capitol which attempted to block ratification of the election which had been won by the Democrat, Joe Biden.

"We got Trump elected"

Troy Newman of Operation Rescue has spoken excitedly about the successes he and his "pro-life" allies had been making to advance conservative causes and enforce restrictions on access to abortion across the United States under President Trump. He boasted:

> *"We got Trump elected - we put a lot of effort into that, we're putting Supreme Court justices in place, and now stacking legislation that is going to end abortion as we know it. I think these guys should be very worried they'll soon end up in jail."*

There are obviously many anti-abortionists who feel strongly about this as their main concern, but there is a hint here that "pro-life" issues have been used by some of the more political actors to boost the conservative bid for power in the US. Newman and other "pro-lifers" are probably very aware that the best way to reduce the number of abortions is to promote good, accessible contraception - something that never makes it into their triumphalist speeches. The crude fact is that for many of them it is conservatism itself, and bringing it to power, which is the goal.

The war over women and unborn foetuses in the US has reached deep into the different levels of government itself. At one point President Trump said that abortion ought to be illegal and that women who undergo such a procedure should face "some sort of punishment". Faced with a barrage of criticism, he retreated by saying that it was the doctors and health staff who should be held criminally responsible. His Vice-President, Mike Pence, and many key political appointments including Ambassador to the United Nations and Secretary of Health, had a track record of opposition to contraception and all forms of pregnancy termination.

During his campaign, Trump created a Catholic advisory group filled with some of the most vehement anti-choice advocates in the US. It included John Klink, who during his time as advisor to the Holy See Mission to the United Nations used his position of influence in the US to ensure that:

> *"the wave of so-called 'reproductive and sexual rights' would [not] be enshrined as new 'fundamental' human rights."*

Another was Austin Ruse, president of the Center for Family and Human Rights (C-Fam), who has stated in regards to anti-abortion issues:

> *"Trump will let our side do exactly what we want to do."*

He was referring mainly to domestic provision for women, but indeed Trump acted quickly on the international scene, "projecting ideology onto global health programs," as Brian Dixon of the Population Connection Action Fund has described it. The result, he predicted, would be the closure of clinics in huge areas of the developing world, with a shortage of medication, increases in diseases like AIDS, malaria and TB, and the unchecked advance of the coronavirus Covid-19. Failure to provide good contraception would also lead to increases in abortion, almost all of it in dangerous circumstances that would cost many women their lives.

Global gags

President Trump's "Global Gag Rule" (officially named "Protecting Life in Global Health Assistance") required any non-governmental organisations that receive US funds to stop providing, referring to, or even sharing information about abortion, even if it is legal in that country and paid from non-US funds. So much for freedom of expression and the Second Amendment to the US Constitution. This is an even more extreme version of a policy first introduced under President Reagan, which had led to the closure of many health services providing basic health and maternity care, often in the poorest and most inaccessible areas. The gag had been removed by President Obama but quickly restored by Trump, then revoked by the new President Biden as one of his first acts after coming into office. A furious row then broke out with most of the US Catholic bishops threatening to withdraw communion from him and any other liberal Catholics who supported family planning.

Since the US is the largest source of humanitarian aid worldwide, and especially since it seeks to silence even those funded by other donors, the Global Gag policy set back health provision across the globe, and especially any help with modern contraception. Aid groups were forced to choose between rigid adherence to the anti-abortion rule for all services, whether funded by the US or not, or giving up on US funding altogether in order to keep their freedom of action. In many cases the loss of funds meant that they had to cancel some of the most important family planning services in the poorest areas. The funding ban, which was supposed to stop abortions, actually increased the rate of abortions by about 40% in the countries studied because of the loss of contraceptive services and therefore the increasing number of unwanted pregnancies. Alongside the gag rule, the US Administration proposed to cut over $600 million in direct funding for family planning, and scrapped the financial contribution to the UN Population Fund (UNFPA). The good news for women is that there has always been opposition in the US Congress, led by the women, to the policies of the "pro-life" movement.

It is hoped that US legislators, and future Administrations, will soften or repeal other measures put through under Bush, Reagan and Trump. As power changes hands in the next few years, however, the battles will continue and policies could shift violently according to which party controls the presidency, the House and the Senate. Given the importance of seniority in both houses of Congress, old conservative attitudes are very hard to shift.

One measure that will be hard for the liberals to remove is the Helms Amendment, dating from George Bush's presidency. This prohibited US aid funds being used for "abortion as a method of family planning" and has been over-interpreted as banning abortion counselling and referrals, post-abortion care, and terminations in cases of rape, incest or a threat to a woman's life. It is the feverish atmosphere around abortion in the US, as well as the amendment itself, which inhibits those on the ground from offering proper care.

Other aid donor countries moved quickly to replace the lost funds from the US Government, although this merely attempted to rescue existing programmes when there was already a desperate need for expansion. Thank you Sweden, Denmark, Finland, Netherlands, Belgium, Luxembourg, Canada and Cape Verde. But much more support was still needed, not just to make up the US funding cuts but to safeguard the non-governmental work and to extend the programmes to all areas. Yet another huge cut in funding has happened with the British Government's enormous cuts to its aid budget, with the 85 % cut in agreed funding for the UN Fund for Population delivering another blow, and cancellation without notice of other excellent and innovative aid projects. The cuts to the supplies programme alone meant that the agency would be unable to prevent an estimated quarter of a million maternal and child deaths, almost 15 million unintended pregnancies, and 4.3 million unsafe abortions. The Gates Foundation and other charitable donors are now making up much of the shortfall here but this underlines the fragility of funding for family planning. Until there is greater understanding of why family planning is so crucial it seems there will be constant battles to maintain the existing services, let alone expand them to meet all the needs.

"We leave it to others"

Faced with the barrage of conservative propaganda and extremism it is very sad, though perhaps not really surprising, that so many western-based women's organisations have turned their backs on the issues of pregnancy and birth, and how we can control the fertility that nature has given us in such abundance. Some feminists cite the supposed feminist leader Germaine Greer, in what is perhaps her most ill-informed book *Sex and Destiny*, where she idealises poor families with many children, misunderstands the contraceptive methods available, argues that the women should not use any form of birth control, and seriously suggests that not having sex would be the answer anyway. Really, Germaine?

In most of the richer countries the battles for family planning have been won, and most women can take for granted that we can have sex without getting pregnant, with the option of the "morning-after" pill or termination at an early stage if contraception fails. Our whole life is managed on the basis that we do not have to be pregnant if we do not want to, and can therefore have as much control over our own lives as men do. However, this security means that we seem to have forgotten what it was like for our mothers and grandmothers not so long ago, when they did not have these easy choices. We either ignore the problems of women who do not have it, or in the case of Germaine Greer and others like her they even argue for double standards: contraception for "us" but not for "them".

While countless column inches and many hours of broadcast time in rich countries are devoted to promoting fertility among women who cannot conceive when they want to, and big money is invested in IVF (in-vitro fertilisation) and fertility research, contraception gets almost no media attention and far too little money. Where there have been political battles in western countries for women's reproductive rights, they have been around abortion. Some activists in the wealthier countries say they do not need to promote contraception because the debate on that is "over" for them. The problem is: for poorer women, especially in the poorer countries, it has hardly begun.

So what about the internationally-based non-governmental organisations? Surely they will be advocating the best possible contraception for all? Unfortunately this is really where the problem lies. Many of them are avoiding the issue, thus offering a perfect excuse for the rest of the international community to do the same. Amnesty International is a particular offender on this: they campaign for abortion rights in different countries but have almost nothing to say about contraception. Some of the big international aid organisations have stopped offering any support for family planning even when they have done it in the past.

Looking just at the UK-based agencies, for example, confusion reigns. Oxfam UK, which used to offer contraceptive services, have now retreated: "We leave it to others," according to a representative I contacted. The problem is, in many of the areas where they work, there are no others (or only the tender mercies of a Catholic clinic or hospital). The Catholic aid agency Cafod predictably offers no help to women on reproductive health. Womankind organises support groups for women in several different countries, but no access to family planning services at all. Save the Children provides contraception, but not abortion. Meanwhile, however, Christian Aid - which itself faces strong negative pressures from some of the churches which support it - courageously asserts:

> *"We believe that reproductive healthcare should be provided in the context of high-quality primary healthcare for women, men and their children."*

So there is no consistency, and for many areas where there are British voluntary aid programmes, any help with planning for children is specifically excluded. It is a pattern too often repeated by aid agencies whether bilateral or multilateral.

International

The women's international lobby sends representatives to UN meetings to raise issues like female genital mutilation (FGM), rape, domestic violence, or women's rights at work, both nationally and internationally. They are often funded and supported by their own governments. Many of them, sadly, have nothing to say about women's rights to decide when to get pregnant, and will try to block any attempts to raise the issue. I contacted the co-ordinating group The Association for Women's Rights in Development (AWID) and it was agreed that I would write a piece about this for their website. Disappointingly - but not surprisingly - it never appeared, there was no further contact with me and their silence on this issue continues. AWID describes itself as "the only international feminist organisation in the world" with member groups in 163 countries. Maintaining international silence about one of the key issues for women seems to be what they are really about. In this respect they are lined up with pro-natalists, fundamentalists and US conservative organisations.

A refusal to discuss the issue is an established pattern with many national and international women's organisations. Often it will be just one or a few individuals within the group who react violently against any discussion of contraception. The strength of opposition among a few means that the majority will back off, and it becomes a subject to be avoided. Since there is such a taboo against discussing the issues, many of them seem to believe that we are still living in a past where indeed there were attempts at "population control" - a discredited approach which no longer prevails. Some of them also, curiously, refuse to use the word "population" at all. I have heard it claimed that to discuss population numbers is somehow "blaming poor women".

Some in these organisations have opposed family planning across the board because unsafe contraceptive trials were allegedly conducted with African women. There is a true double standard here since they are not suggesting that western women should boycott contraception for that reason. There is also a notion that contraception is uniquely dangerous to a woman who is malnourished. I had one conversation with a leading international feminist where she came out with this last one. I pointed out that the most dangerous thing for this woman would actually be pregnancy, especially if it was unwanted. This seemed to be a completely new idea for her. To her credit, she was open to reviewing her approach to the issue, which she had not thought about since the 1970s. If only all the women involved would do the same.

Distracted, overwhelmed, defensive

Although this is largely about wilful avoidance of this topic I do have some sympathy with AWID and other women's groups, even though I disagree. If we try to understand why this avoidance is happening, we have to acknowledge the huge range of issues the women's organisations are facing in advancing and defending women's rights while trying to make women central to development. Their attention is increasingly being focused on the horrors of war for women - especially the murder, rape, kidnap and enslavement of women which is increasingly a part of modern warfare. The horrible conditions for many women and their children who are refugees from war is another cause for concern. Then there are the single-issue campaigns like female genital mutilation (FGM), sexual exploitation, domestic violence or forced marriage, all of which are seen to have a better chance of success than tackling all the issues at once.

Defending the rights of lesbians and transsexuals has also become important, as have the rights of sex workers. Community activism, the environment and opposition to harmful development, especially for indigenous people, is a particular focus for some women's groups. All of these are important issues. However they should not obscure the importance for women in bad situations of at least being able to avoid bringing another baby into a conflict-ridden world where they cannot even guarantee their own safety, or that of the children they already have.

Women's rights advocates in some developing countries are also facing a right-wing backlash aimed at reversing hard-won rights. There have been murders and death threats to women who are human rights defenders. These have caused great concern throughout the movement, which feels an urgent need to support and defend these activists. Much effort has had to be spent on defending the advances already made, and for many groups in Third World countries the challenge is merely to survive.

This is also about money: who has it and who does not. All the international women's organisations are financially weak, and all too conscious that their limited budgets are a fraction of the money available to the big development agencies and the environmental organisations, who often have big money from philanthopists. There has been an overall decrease in funding to women's organisations from official bilateral and multilateral aid agencies which arose from the 2008 global financial crisis, the increasing numbers of conservative governments, and public pressure in the rich countries to reduce foreign aid for developing countries. At the same time the efforts of many have shifted from campaigning on global issues to working in their particular areas on practical projects, as women and girls become recognised as central to the global development agenda. Economic issues dominate: land rights, legal issues, access to education, finance, markets and working conditions. All of these are important, but the fact that none of this will work if women cannot control the number and timing of their children has not been sufficiently considered.

Not rocking the boat

The reality is that many women in the international voluntary organisations are tired, distracted and overwhelmed. The energy needed for a rethink on reproductive issues is just not there for some of the most hard-pressed. Some of them, especially in the richer countries, have lost their open-mindedness and their campaigning edge as their organisations become more professionalised. They were originally set up and run mainly by committed volunteers who could say what they liked, but now there are paid staff, often young and insecure, occupying jobs in international development for which there is fierce competition. They have money to earn, rent to pay, their own children to support, careers to nurture. Are they going to rock the boat? If there is no support from other colleagues but hostility from some others? Or if they go to a conference and face a fierce attack by another individual or organisation accusing them of wanting "population control"? The answer too often is: no way. Not me, let someone else do it.

Such debates can become vicious and intensely personal. There are a few organisations which have close ties to the "pro-lifers" and have the money to attend all the international conferences. One such organisation loudly proclaims projects such as "the Virtual Mural for Abortion Rights!" (everything comes with a "!") but also "attacks the population control mentality and the development of contraceptive vaccines from a feminist point of view". It is doubtful whether women facing unmanageable pregnancies would agree that this is a pro-women or feminist point of view.

I was struck at a recent conference on women in development that there were frequent mentions of unwanted pregnancies by the young Third World women present, but absolutely no comment on what they had said, or on the issue itself, from the more established delegates representing mainly US bodies. Women from the South have a better understanding of this than those based in the North who insist that they cannot discuss the issue. Younger women understand better than older and more senior ones.

This taboo is blocking what could be life-saving work. There seems to be little awareness among many women's organisations of the hugely beneficial impact that women's groups on the ground can have if they work together for family planning and sexual health. As Women and Children First concludes, women's groups working on these issues in poor areas can transform lives:

> *"Where at least 30% of pregnant women took part in the groups, maternal deaths can be reduced by up to 49% and newborn deaths by a third."*

With such dramatic improvements in lives saved, it is ironic that women in so many national and international organisations - who themselves would not dream of giving up their own choices about sexuality and whether to have children - are turning their backs on the issue just when their support is most needed. Double standards for rich and poor women are all too prevalent, and simply not acceptable.

The women's movement - like other radical movements - has always had bitter disputes, as individuals try to become "holier than thou" on various topics, which means denouncing others while bystanders maintain an uneasy silence. If you experience even one of these you carry the scars with you, and tend to avoid other potential confrontations. It is all too easy for the Antis to put women off even mentioning fertility issues, let alone having a proper discussion. And so it is that much of the international, western-based women's movement - which should be leading the campaign for family planning worldwide - maintains a rigid silence on the subject.

"Talking about it became taboo"

There are, of course, important exceptions to the avoidance of family planning issues. Many women's organisations in poor countries, notably in Latin America and the Caribbean, have been vociferous in their demands for contraception and a general opening up of health services to the poorest women. There are voluntary family planning associations working tirelessly in almost every country in the world to introduce clinic services and to lobby their own local authorities and governments to fund these on a bigger scale. They are backed by a network of international support organisations which include their own International Planned Parent Federation (IPPF) and the United Nations Fund for Population (UNFPA) together with many national and international bodies specifically working to improve women's access to services. They have been joined by a few very big private donors, including the Gates Foundation which channels some of the billions of Microsoft founder Bill Gates and ex-wife Melinda. They are supporting family planning programmes in some of the poorest countries with the least support, and financing research and lobbying work. All of these are campaigning for understanding and support on contraception and sexual health as an integral element in international development.

These organisations do brilliant work, developing contraception delivery and outreach while monitoring outcomes and researching the needs and the issues. In 2015 they finally managed, after many years of trying and failing, to get reproductive health as one of the UN's Sustainable Development Goals (SDGs) for international development, with the target by 2030 to:

> *"ensure universal access to sexual and reproductive health-care services, including for family planning, information and education, and the integration of reproductive health into national strategies and programmes."*

It was a great leap forward. Constant work will still be needed, though, to make sure it is implemented.

The "population" organisations, especially the US-based ones, often use the word "population" in their names - anathema to those on the other side, which does not help communication. They tend to live within a bubble where everyone agrees, even if "outsiders" do not. They are not communicating enough with development economists and practitioners, the international health and "One Health" sector, or environmentalists. The population people campaign with, and speak to, mainly other specialist groups in their own field. My immersion in their social media conversations reveals a morass of jargon and initials which they understand but are never explained, and which no outsider would know. This includes the key term "SRHR" (sexual and reproductive health and rights) which is not well understood or supported in general development circles or the wider world. I regularly find almost impenetrable language being used, like this classic from the online magazine *SRHM (Sexual and Reproductive Health Matters)*:

> *"SRHR accountability research must address including social and political contextualisation of accountability, unpacking the operations of power, the context of community driven accountability interventions and addressing marginalisation through accountability research."*

Clear communication? If only.

In the closet

The family planning organisations have generally failed to engage with women's groups, even to the extent of keeping them informed of the advances in their field such as new contraceptive methods or successful project models. They collectively give the impression of staying in their comfort zone, preaching to the converted and staying well away from the nasty opposition.

This insularity is feeding the taboos against discussion. Martha Campbell, who has been centrally involved in all of this, has described the current situation as "a perfect storm of silence" adopted by family planning organisations as a way to preserve services, but which in reality has lost them vital support. She points to the run-up to the 1994 Cairo conference (UN International Conference on Population and Development, or ICPD).

> *"Talking about population became politically incorrect in many circles. Drawing attention to any connection between population*

growth and environmental destruction became taboo..."

At a time when the family planning community is under extreme pressure over funding and support, it is crucial that they break the silence.

Can we look forward to a time when the international women's movement campaigns for women's right to decide whether to have children, and when? We live in hope. But as my mother used to say, grimly, we die in despair. The optimistic view of this would be that they - and international development specialists - perhaps needed to go through a rejection of the old ideas of a "population explosion" focused purely on overall numbers, and come to a more humanitarian view that stresses the importance of enabling individual choices about having children, particularly for women.

The opposition - the Global Gag advocates - are on a self-defined "crusade" to stop abortion and/or contraception. Many advocates of women's rights are too ready to retreat in the face of such determination and aggression, and their readiness to accuse others of advocating "population control", "eugenics" and the rest. Here then is perhaps the true explanation of the unwillingness of the international women's movement to discuss fertility issues: it is the Adamants versus the Avoiders. The Adamants are aggressive, spoiling for a fight. The Avoiders are timid, careerist, and back away from confrontation.

While working on this, I am continually reminded of the poet WB Yeats's lines from his poem "The Second Coming" written in 1919 during the build-up to the horrific civil war in Ireland:

> *"The best lack all conviction, while the worst*
> *"Are full of passionate intensity."*

We are not talking about a war, of course, unless you see this as a war on women. But the injuries, the suffering and loss of life from unwanted pregnancies and damaged mothers and babies is on an even greater scale.

We should try to counter the "passionate intensity" of the fundamentalists, the Holy See and other pro-natalists with a conviction of our own that family planning is the ultimate life saver, and a key part of any work to relieve poverty and enable all women to achieve their full potential, wherever they live.

"An old, smelly dog"

In the 1960s and 1970s several environmental writers warned of the "population explosion" or "Population Bomb" as described in Paul and Anne Ehrlich's influential book of that name published in 1968. There have been others, with titles like "Full House", "10 Billion", "Hot, Flat and Crowded", and "Peoplequake", which tend towards a panic over numbers rather than the issues facing individuals. The "Worldometer" website even has a ticking set of numbers which purport to show the numbers of births per second worldwide, and "population growth in the world" of ticking births compare with ticking deaths. It fosters a feeling of panic, and panic is never a good approach to solving the really big problems of the world.

Environmentalists have backed away from previous concerns about population, and I can only conclude that - like the women's organisations - many have simply backed away from unpleasant confrontations. According to the veteran campaigner Dave Foreman, *"overpopulation worry is kicked into the corner and shunned like an old, smelly dog."*

Take the near-civil war within the Sierra Club in the United States. Previously strongly supportive of work to help people stabilise their family size, its Board was infiltrated in the 1990s by white supremacists with overtly racist views, who wanted to turn this into an anti-immigration campaign.

Larry Fahn, Sierra Club president during some of the bitterest infighting, explained:

"When you talk about population, the immigration people come out of the woodwork with their hate mongering. It's unfortunate that the subject brings out a racist agenda."

The outcome was a virtual prohibition on discussion of human population increase and its impact on the environment. The organisation failed to take the more effective approach would have been to tackle the question of people's decisions about children without allowing it to be linked to immigration issues. It is a mistake that several groups have made in the past. Migration is an important topic and should be discussed, but separately - not in the context of people taking life and death decisions about children.

The link between human numbers and the natural environment is obvious - some might say the elephant in the room. Environmentalists have had to look hard for excuses for their avoidance of the issue. Some of these go beyond even what the western women's groups are saying. The "deep green" writer George Monbiot, while claiming that western over-consumption is the only cause of environmental destruction and climate change, has even written that highlighting women's rights, the need for family planning and the expanding human population means "blaming the victims". He has claimed that those who accept the connections are "obsessed" (unlike him, of course, with his regular attacks on them).

"Population bomb"

These (mainly male) environmentalists do have one obvious get-out clause, of course: that the international women's movement has failed to raise the issues effectively. Some of the men have even described the women as "pro-natalist" although this is certainly an exaggeration. Apart from Germaine Greer the women's groups are not advocating more births, they are avoiding the issue altogether. It is far too easy (and dishonest) for the environmental movement, which is enormously big, professional, well-financed and powerful, to blame the struggling women's organisations for their own inadequacies.

It is very unfortunate that the key book on this topic, Anne and Paul Ehrlich's *Population Bomb*, has in the end proved counter-productive in trying to get environmentalist to focus on the issue. The book predicted worldwide famine in the 1970s which would kill hundreds of millions of people. Predictions are always risky and this one did not happen - or at least not on the scale they suggested. Even more serious than this was their advocacy of the now abandoned policy of "population control," including forcing Indian men who had three or more children to be sterilized, or offering financial incentives without proper information. This has allowed many to dismiss their and other people's warnings about human population increases, and to ridicule any notion that large numbers of people could ever run out of food.

Some claim that technological advances will be developed to allow ever-increasing numbers of people to be fed. They may add that the more babies are born, the more chance there is of one of them finding the answer (by the poorest people with the least education?). Many still argue that environmental destruction is purely a problem of over-consumption by rich consumers, despite some very persuasive analysis by colleagues showing that the increasing numbers of very poor people are also a major factor in many areas, especially those with the most fragile ecologies and need for conservation. Indeed, the desperation of people without land, employment or place in society is driving them to take over and degrade huge areas of land previously left to wildlife and nature, such as rainforests and semi-deserts - precisely the areas that environmentalists are so worried about. Poor landless people may also have no real choice about working for the landowners who invade wild areas to grow soya or oil palm, or keep beef cattle for sale to richer western countries.

Another favoured argument, especially among the men, is that synthetic oestrogens in some hormonal contraceptives are getting into the rivers via sewage treatment plants, and may interfere with the reproduction of some fish. I am waiting for these men to campaign for the obvious alternative of barrier methods which do not use hormones, including condoms and male sterilisation. Most of them would not even be using barrier methods themselves. Instead: leave it to the women, and then let's blame them!

There is probably some truth in the claim about oestrogen, although the widely used chemical Bisphenol A is also suspected of having this effect on fish. The definitive environmental answer to the anti-hormone argument has been humorously but clearly set out by Umbra Fisk in the online environmental magazine *Grist*. She argues that effective contraception is so vital to individuals and the planet that it offsets even some environmental damage.

> *"Preventing the creation of another resource-using, carbon-emitting human is by far the eco-friendliest step anyone can take, even if you create a tower of condom wrappers to do so… Just go forth and <u>don't</u> be fruitful."*

She discusses different methods in some detail, balancing effectiveness as well as environmental effects, and recommends the latest intrauterine devices (IUDs) while "still, given how well it works, the Pill and its ilk remain a viable option". Is this controversial stuff? No, it is environmental common sense. It is a balancing of risks and responsibilities in the best interests of people and the planet.

"Is it sensitivity or cowardice?"

The avoidance of human population issues by so many in the environmental movement has been described by Professor Roger Martin as:

> *"telling a silent lie every time they put out a statement on some environmental problem where they know that every additional person makes it harder and ultimately impossible to solve."*

As with the women's organisations, he finds a partial explanation in the increasing professionalisation of the field. As the previous head of an environmental organisation himself,

> *"when I started with a staff of three, I was a hard-hitting campaigner with a lot of volunteers. By the time I finished ten*

> *years later with a staff of 35, my priority concern, if I'm honest,*
> *had switched from preserving the wildlife of Somerset to keeping*
> *my staff and myself in work. So not upsetting funders became*
> *more and more important, and it made us ever more toothless*
> *watchdogs. And I think that's happened to the Sierra Club*
> *and many others. They've become part of the Establishment,*
> *they don't rock boats."*

The desperation to hold on to funding by avoiding anything controversial is also emphasised by Ed Barry of the US Population Institute:

> *"Many conservation and nongovernmental organizations that*
> *run on member support, even the big ones, shy away from the*
> *population issue. That's because it puts their funding at risk."*

Sadly, the scramble for money has overwhelmed their integrity.

The fact that the environmental movement is very male-dominated also means they are embarrassed about discussing women, especially women's bodies, sexuality and birth. In documentaries about nature they are very happy to show pictures of animals mating, but cannot bring themselves to discuss sex and reproduction among humans. Jonathan Porritt, another leading environmentalist, has explained:

> *"Population raises all these questions about religion, about*
> *culture, about male dominance in the world; and [we] get very*
> *uncomfortable about that."*

George Monbiot has also admitted that human population is:

> *"an important issue most Greens will not discuss. Is this*
> *sensitivity or is it cowardice? Perhaps a bit of both."*

And so the great avoidance of this issue becomes ever more entrenched - even though many of those involved are not even quite sure why, and perhaps are afraid to ask. The old accusing slogans of "eugenics" and "population control" are often put out there, a bit like waving garlic and a cross in front of the female witches, zombies and vampires in horror movies. These words help to build convenient "straw men": pretending that promoting choice is somehow evil and so worthy of contempt and attack. Setting up a "straw man" in an argument is pretending the other side is saying something it is not, constructing a weak position that you claim they hold and then proceeding to demolish it. It is deeply dishonest, and it is embedded in the anti-choice position. Take, for example, a statement from the London-based Friends of the Earth:

> *"There are good grounds… for being sceptical about the efficacy of 'population control' campaigns."*

There are no such campaigns, dear FoE, with the single exception of the Chinese Government's "one/ two/ three children" policy.

Thriving Together

Fortunately, even Friends of the Earth have recently turned away from their previous position after a lot of work was done to educate and inform them. The big environmental organisations are still stuck mainly on the "avoidance" side of the argument but change is happening, although very slowly. The leading broadcaster David Attenborough, who has always refused to accept that consumption in rich countries is the only threat to the environment, has put it simply:

> *"All our environmental problems become easier to solve with fewer people and harder - and ultimately impossible to solve - with ever more people."*

The leading environmental theorist Lester Pearson has

written extensively on the issues in *Full Planet, Empty Plates* and other books. Frederic Ballenegger, an environmental and ethical philosopher, argues:

> *"Grossly unsustainable consumption patterns in the industrialized world, combined with uncontrolled demographic growth in the least developed countries and elsewhere, lead to the destruction of habitat and species, which is ethically indefensible... Having acquired the means to destroy creation, humans also gained the duty to preserve it, including its diversity."*

In June 2012, at the Rio+20 Conference, a statement was issued by the combined non-governmental environmental organisations saying that:

> *"stable populations are an essential part of any sustainable future... reducing our personal footprint does not help if we keep increasing the number of feet - we need to limit both."*

The United Nations Under-Secretary-General, Thoraya Ahmed Obaid, added:

> *"We cannot confront the massive challenges of poverty, hunger, disease and environmental destruction unless we address issues of population and reproductive health."*

Some important conservation organisations which are working in the most sensitive areas for wildlife are now introducing a health and family planning element for the people whose support they need if the programmes are to succeed. One of the pioneers in "Population Health and Environment" (PHE) work is Blue Ventures, who focus on marine wildlife conservation in partnership with fishing communities. There are now others, working to preserve a wide variety of threatened species while also improving the lives and prospects of people in the area concerned. The

Margaret Pyke Trust and the Population and Sustainability Network are working to inform and involve environmentalists, to help them set up PHE projects, and to bring up the issues at key conferences.

These are all steps in the right direction, and it could be that the environmental conservation movement will emerge as the leaders in bringing family planning to people who have so far been beyond the reach of national programmes. We need many more such moves before the environmental movement is fully committed to helping everyone to plan for their children.

The Thriving Together initiative in 2019 brought together conservation and family planning advocates working in 170 countries with the statement:

> *"If we come together and engage in what we call 'Healthy Thinking', we believe partnerships across the health and environment sectors can create the prosperous future for people and nature that everyone wants."*

The list of conservation organisations involved is particularly striking - from Africa Youth for SDGs and Amphibian Ark to many of the zoos around the world. There are more of them based in Africa than in any other region. The International Union for Conservation of Nature and Natural Resources (IUCN), the world's largest and most diverse environmental network with a membership of governments, big NGOs and indigenous organisations, saw a landslide victory for its keynote resolution in November 2020:

> *"Importance for the conservation of nature of removing barriers to rights-based voluntary family planning"* ("Motion 087").

Support for the motion came from all regions of the world and all categories of governments and non-governmental organisations, and it is striking that every indigenous body voted in favour.

Environmentalists are finally moving on this issue, and could end up taking the lead. Let us hope that the international women's movement, and the development economists, decide to join them.

Resources

Pope Francis, *Amoris Laetitia* ("Joy of Love") 2016.

Beth Holloway, "Circulatory Changes at Birth", URMC Online Medical Encyclopedia.

Michelle Goldberg, *The Means of Reproduction: Sex, Power, and the Future of the World* (Penguin Press, New York, 2009).

Diane J Horvath-Cosper, "Being a doctor who performs abortions means you always fear your life is in danger," Washington Post, 29 October 2015. Also various news reports in US news services and publications.

Troy Newman quoted in "Late-Stage Abortion Provider Won't Succumb to Protesters Who Forced Him Out of His Last Maryland Clinic," by Rachel M Cohen (*The Intercept*, online, 30 October 2017).

Llyse Hogue, "Becket Fund: Shadow Agents of the Religious Right," *Conscience* online magazine, US Catholics for Choice, 6 May 2021

Germaine Greer, *Sex and Destiny: The Politics of Human Fertility* (Harper Collins, London, 1984).

Srilatha Batliwala, AWID Scholar Associate, "Beyond individual stories: women have moved mountains," Open Democracy website, 18 February 2013.

Angelika Arutyonova, "Starving the roots of women's human

rights groups," Open Democracy website, 6 December 2013.

Martha Campbell, "Why the Silence on Population?" in Philip Cafaro and Eileen Crist (eds), *Life on the Brink: Environmentalists Confront Overpopulation* (University of Georgia Press, US, 2012).

Paul R Ehrlich, *The Population Bomb* (Sierra Club and Ballantine Books, 1968, republished by Buccaneer Books, 1971). Anne Ehrlich was a co-author but omitted from the title after pressure from the publisher.

Lester R Brown, *Full Planet, Empty Plates: The new geopolitics of food scarcity* (W W Norton, 2012)

Philip Cafaro and Eileen Crist (eds), *Life on the Brink: Environmentalists Confront Overpopulation* (University of Georgia Press, 2012).

Frederic Ballenegger, "The Ethics and Theology of Population Dynamics," Harvard University Research Paper, December 2012.

Umbra Fisk, "Ask Umbra," in online environmental magazine *Grist*, 30 May 2016.

Interview with Roger Martin on *Grist*, 27 October 2011.

Chapter seven

WORLDWIDE: PRO-NATALISTS ON THE WARPATH

Never underestimate the power of organised religion when it is committed to a single project. This is certainly true of the Catholic Church, which has campaigned relentlessly to stop women and men choosing when to have children. Its campaign is not confined to its own members (about one in seven of the world's people) but seeks to impose this dogma on the whole world.

The vehicle for their influence is their pseudo-state, the Vatican. Its status is dubious, and its diplomatic presence worldwide is based on a fallacy that this is a State. The Vatican is now known internationally as the "Holy See", which is the official bureaucracy of this tiny area of Rome - smaller and less significant in reality than a small local authority. The Vatican itself is also a recent invention, not even a historical relic. It was created in 1929 by the Lateran Treaty between the Catholic Church and the then Italian head of state, the fascist leader Benito Mussolini. This is not the image they like to create of themselves as an ancient and unchanging State.

Pope John Paul II, meeting there with Vladimir Putin in 2003, acknowledged:

> *"What kind of state do I have here? You can see my whole state right from this window."*

Its total area is smaller than a standard-sized golf course. Unlike any national or local authority it has no permanent residents, who could be considered citizens, only church employees who have to leave when their contract is ended. Nobody who lives or works there has citizenship or voting rights. The Holy See/ Vatican issues no passports to anyone except "diplomatic" ones. The area is inhabited almost entirely by men, most of whom have no wives or children. The very few women living and working there are mainly nuns, who are celibate and also have no children. If any children are born to people working there they have to be citizens of another country.

There is no democratically elected government or local authority. Many of the basic municipal functions are carried out by the Government of Italy and municipality of Rome, including water and sewage, power supplies and rubbish collection, policing of the area and prosecuting any crimes committed there. The Vatican has some decorative "Swiss Guards" - historically a group of mercenaries but later committed by the Swiss Government from its own army to the Pope's exclusive use. They have largely ceremonial duties inside the area, their official function being to protect him and his cardinals personally rather than to control the Vatican as a whole.

When is a State not a State?

The Holy See/ Vatican is not able to meet the criteria for a State under the 1933 Montevideo Convention on the Rights and Duties of States, one of the requirements being a permanent population. It refuses to ratify many human rights treaties and other international agreements. Yet this strange entity has now managed to get its own unique place at the United Nations as a "non-member State Permanent Observer" with free access to almost all meetings and their documentation, a free pass to the Delegates' Lounge, other bars and offices in the building, and even its own office at UN headquarters in New York which no country's delegation has.

The "Holy See" is also the only religious body which is being given privileges as if it was a member State at the United Nations. All other world religions have the status of non-governmental organisations, apart from the Islamic world which is emulating the Catholics and starting up the ladder of accreditation, as we shall see later.

With a large and very effective Holy See "diplomatic corps" operating at all international meetings and conferences, as well as behind the scenes, and with ambassadors accredited to 178 countries of the world, the Holy See/ Vatican may not be a State, but it claims many of the privileges of UN membership in order to operate as an extremely powerful and effective lobbying machine. That lobbying power is directed mainly at opposing the case for human rights to include women's rights, and women's rights to include the right to choose when or whether to have children.

Obviously the Catholic Church and its Holy See/ Vatican are not the only opponents of family planning, but their influence has been so great on so many levels, from individual to international, that they require particular scrutiny. That has been strangely lacking, partly perhaps because of their "holier than thou" aura and the reluctance of many international observers to criticise a religious organisation. Since much of the influence is wielded behind the scenes it can also be difficult to know exactly what its representatives are doing. At the same time they are seen, especially in the UN specialised agencies, as a menacing force that can break the careers of any officials who oppose them and their particular agenda. They can also threaten the agencies' funding if they step out of line, especially by their influence on the US administration and Congress. There seems to be a reluctance among officials of the UN and its agencies to even discuss the issue, since you can never be sure who might be listening.

Use of the Holy See/ Vatican status also means that its influence can grow internationally as the United Nations and its agencies become increasingly central in determining social and economic development goals and practices. This means that the Catholic Church can effectively impose its doctrines on the more than six billion people around the world who are not members, as well as the estimated one billion who are - something no other religion is able to do. This is defiance of the church's own Declaration on Religious Freedom, which states that Catholics must respect the beliefs of people of other faiths, accept that others are acting in accordance with their own conscience, and avoid "any hint of coercion" in spreading their own religious faith and practices.

We should accept that the Catholic Church has the right to proclaim its own doctrine to its own believers on the question of sexuality, women's rights, modern contraception and abortion. Whether church members abide by that is another matter - most of them do not, given the choice. We even have to recognise that as an issue of "infallibility", it is difficult for the current hierarchy to backtrack on their position, however wrong or even immoral it may be. That is also a matter for the Church as a whole.

It is ironic that the Catholic Church's doctrinal insistence on promoting births is more powerfully achieved at the political and international level than it is among its own members through the power of their moral authority and preaching. The hierarchy's influence within the church itself – through priests, bishops, archbishops and cardinals - is overshadowed by the formidable force that is the Vatican's political strength and its diplomatic service. Here the opposition to protected sex is based on the most conservative interpretation of doctrine, built up largely through the hierarchy's preference for promoting its most hard-line adherents from the ranks of ordinary priests, and carried forward by powerful individual men who make this a particular personal cause. There are plenty of contradictions in the theological teachings, highlighted by Pope Benedict's guarded approval of condoms as a "first step" in the fight against AIDS while at the same time the Holy See still opposes their inclusion in international anti-AIDS programmes. Despite Benedict's ruling the provision of condoms is still prohibited in the vast Catholic network of HIV/ AIDS clinics, although there are rumours of some staff there handing them out secretly.

It is an extraordinary situation, especially when we recall that the Catholic doctrine of opposition to contraception is an invention of the late 19th century, as we have seen, and nothing to do with original Church teachings either from Christ himself or over the first nineteen centuries of the Church's existence. In this chapter we take a look at their use of lobbying power to block people's access to choice through family planning.

Uninvited guests

Now a fixture on the international scene, giving the appearance of something perhaps rooted in antiquity, the Holy See/ Vatican's status is in fact a very recent invention, the product of clever manoeuvering from 1929 onwards. In that year it reached a definitive Concordat agreement with Mussolini's Fascist government in Italy, through the Lateran Treaty, which recognised the full sovereignty of the Holy See in Vatican City, and this still governs its legal position today.

In 1933 the Vatican agreed another Concordat, with the Fascists in Germany, agreeing not to oppose Hitler's power in return for being allowed to run Catholic schools and youth movement without interference. The Holy See/ Vatican then began to push hard for membership of international organisations before and after World War 2, with a particular emphasis on negotiations to establish the World Health Organisation (WHO) after the war.

Amazingly, considering how aggressively the Holy See has operated within the United Nations, there is absolutely no legal basis for its presumed status at the UN, its specialised agencies and its development-related conferences:

no resolution of the General Assembly or Security Council, and no record of any other decision. Its attempt to join the League of Nations between the wars had been rejected and it reportedly "regretted its exclusion". This was largely due to scepticism about its claims to be a State, and the possibility that it would have undue influence on the votes of member States with mainly Catholic populations.

In 1944 the Holy See made tentative inquiries to the United States about the eligibility of "Vatican City" to join the future United Nations, and was told by the then Secretary of State, Cordell Hull:

> *"The Vatican would not be capable of fulfilling all the responsibilities of membership."*

However Vatican City had been able to join the World Telegraph Union (now the International Telecommunications Union) and the Universal Postal Union before World War II, being able to print and sell its own postage stamps. When the United Nations was being set up after the war this was used by the Vatican as a precedent to gain admission into UN meetings, although it would be only as an observer.

In 1948 the Food and Agriculture Organisation of the UN (FAO), which is based in Rome and so had connections to the Vatican, became the first specialised UN agency to grant "Holy See/ Vatican City" the status of Permanent Observer to conferences. A few others followed with Vatican representatives attending meetings, sometimes by invitation but at other times without any accreditation. They had a particular interest in the World Health Organisation, which they had earlier threatened to undermine by setting up their own international Catholic health body if the WHO promoted family planning. As a result the WHO committed itself to excluding contraceptive services from its programmes, and is still unwilling to integrate family planning into its worldwide health projects. Since the WHO is the critical agency dealing with health internationally, the impact of this failure has been substantial.

It was not until 1964 that the then Secretary-General of the United Nations, U Thant, accepted the Holy See's self-designation as a Permanent Observer to the UN itself. Since he would not have taken any major decisions without consulting the US and Soviet Union, and since the Soviets may not have had a position on it, the Americans in particular would certainly have instructed him to move in that direction.

In 2004 the Holy See was granted the right to speak freely in all debates, the right of reply to any other interventions, and the right to have their own documents circulated to all member States. There is no record of the General Assembly or the Security Council making any such decision. It was another back-door deal, with the conservative Catholic bishops' lobby using their influence with the United States Government to leverage a presence at the heart of the United Nations. The President in 2004 was George W Bush, and this was his mid-term election year. It was an ideal opportunity for the bishops to extract concessions from him as the price of their support for his re-election, with no publicity and no political price to be paid domestically.

According to the UN's International Law Commission,

> "...observers were accepted only from non-member States which were full members of one or more specialized agencies and were generally recognized by Members of the United Nations."

Since the Holy See's acceptance was never put to meetings of the members, this could not have been established. This is in contract to the other non-member observer, the State of Palestine, which was given that status through a General Assembly resolution.

Interestingly, Pope John Paul II confirmed that the Holy See had not been invited into international bodies but had invited itself:

> *"Pope Paul VI initiated the formal participation of the Holy See in the United Nations Organization."*

Search and destroy

This is critically important because of the use or abuse by the Holy See of its status at international meetings, especially those related to international development, human rights and specifically the rights of women. Unlike all other Observers at the UN, the Holy See is now automatically invited by the Secretariat to attend UN conferences and participate with "all the privileges of a State," even including the supposed right to vote, even though there is no basis for this in international law. I have seen for myself how anxious UN employees are to take copies of all documents to the Holy See office, because they are so quick to complain about them personally if they are late.

The Holy See has used this situation relentlessly to scrutinise all proposals and object to even the smallest details. As Catholics for Choice point out:

> *"The official documents from UN conferences on women and population and development are replete with objections to the majority consensus made by representatives of the Holy See."*

They are also experts at the small print and using procedural rules to obstruct proposals. They will challenge any reference to women's rights, and the right to sexual health and family planning.

Much of the influence wielded by the Vatican and Holy See, especially in the early days, was achieved by lobbying officials, delegations and individual governments rather than submitting to votes by member-States, and there is no doubt that this is still continuing. Stephen Mumford reveals that at the International Population Conference in Mexico City in 1984 the Vatican achieved its goals through the United States delegation, which was made up largely of conservative Catholics appointed by then President Ronald Reagan. The US delegation took the official Vatican policy on abortion and family planning and helped to impose it on the meeting.

This was followed by the key Cairo Conference in 1994, when the US delegation was more broadly based and no longer represented the hierarchy's position. The Vatican then had to come out from behind the screens and act in its own case. Everyone was stunned when the Holy See managed to shut down the whole meeting for its first six days. They then proceeded to challenge and obstruct every attempt to introduce the right to family planning. In desperation, the Chair of the meeting suspended discussions and, against all the usual procedures, invited representatives of all the non-governmental organisations present onto the conference floor to speak to the delegates.

At the 1995 Beijing Conference on Women large sections of the final report had to be put in brackets, meaning they were not approved by consensus, even though State representatives had all agreed it. It was the Holy See that had objected to these provisions, including the entire section on health, claiming that the text gave

> *"totally unbalanced attention to sexual and reproductive health"*

and condemning family planning as "morally unacceptable". They were able to use their anomalous position within the conference to veto decisions reached by representatives of all the world's governments.

"Like a hungry man eating food"

Those of us who are not Catholics - the great majority of the world's people - should not accept that the church, via the "Holy See", has the right to invite itself into the United Nations without any legal basis, to exploit their access to the maximum and to scrutinise every document, every proposal and every debate in order to block family planning and the women's rights agenda as a whole. They should not be dedicating their diplomatic and lobbying machine to this, nor funding it, nor putting pressure on the UN and specialised agency secretariats, individuals and governments.

In short, they should call off the attack dogs and focus on their legitimate missions of justice and peace, leading moral campaigns on the international stage against poverty and war, and for human rights across the world. Yet the hierarchy has run out of control on this. They already have this UN status, they exploit it to the full, and it could be difficult to dislodge them. It will probably be up to governments to look into this situation and to confront them officially on this, but in the meantime it is important for us to make it better known.

The Holy See machine does not just operate in international organisations, important though these are since this is where world standards are set and development objectives agreed. Many countries with strong Catholic identities have been subjected to extreme pressure from the hierarchies in their own countries to block family planning, women's rights and even sex education. The Philippines recently emerged from decades of bitter battles with the Catholic bishops to pass a Reproductive Health Bill in 2013.

The same is true of Ireland, where the Church controlled social and health policy for years even though it was funded by the Irish State to provide the services. The result has been excessive levels of sickness, disability and death which were unacceptable in any modern country.

In 2012, for example, a desperately ill woman in Galway, Savita Halappanavar, was allowed to die after she was refused a termination on the grounds that "this is a Catholic country" – even though this was in a State hospital and not one of the many private Catholic ones. This notorious case played a role in the overwhelming vote to repeal Ireland's near-total ban on abortion in 2018.

Almost the whole of Latin America is still in the grip of these battles. Michelle Goldberg offers a detailed description of Catholic bishops' pressure on the governments of Costa Rica and Nicaragua, and its devastating effects for many women. The continent-wide network of liberal Catholic groups, Catolicas por el Derecho a Decidir, issued a statement "stained by indignation and sadness" describing:

> *"the profound desire of a masculine church that feels the right to decide and choose what women want or should do with their lives,"*

and in particular a model of the ideal woman whose mission has to include sacrifice, suffering and passivity.

The emergence of the Zika virus, with its devastating effects on foetuses, especially in Brazil, highlighted the issue even more as women were being denied contraception and safe abortion, and forced to bear babies with microcephaly (undeveloped brains) and other severe birth defects. The World Health Organisation developed a Zika strategic response plan that would include family planning and education, but the $122m required to put it into practice was simply not there.

Dr Vincent DeGennaro, who runs a women's health clinic in Haiti, told a reporter from *The Guardian*:

> *"When we are in clinic and we offer women access to birth control they accept it like a hungry man eating food. We are failing women, and with the low cost of contraception, it's hard to say it's not deliberate."*

Giselle Carino of IPPF has commented:

> *"The unfinished sexual and reproductive health and rights agenda has now become a humanitarian crisis in Latin America."*

Captured by Catholics

Catholic bishops and the hierarchy generally have a powerful influence over the United States federal government, even though Catholics are only a fifth of the US population at most (and many of these are of Catholic heritage but not practising). This influence is important because the US Government has a particularly powerful voice in the UN system, as a superpower and the largest UN contributor and aid donor in the world. It is also because the headquarters of the United Nations itself, several specialised agencies, World Bank and IMF are on its territory and within its cultural atmosphere, including the American media. It pays and (for long periods) withholds big financial contributions to the UN itself and its specialised agencies, with delays and outright cuts often caused by opposition to the funding allocations in Congress but more recently ordered by President Trump.

The dead hand of US on/ off contributions creates artificial crises within these organisations, while also imposing various policy restrictions on their activities. Because of the separation of powers entrenched in its Constitution, and almost permanent election cycles, the US is peculiarly susceptible to special interest lobbying, especially on foreign affairs. Given enough single-mindedness, skilled lobbyists, plenty of money and a large and well-organised membership, US government policy can be turned in a particular direction quite easily. The Catholic hierarchy can exert powerful pressure on the President, House of Representatives and Senate, often by threatening that Catholics, their orders and organisations will withdraw election funding and urge their members to vote them out if they do not follow an ultra-conservative line. In 2021 some of the US bishops threatened to exclude Biden and other supporters of reproductive choice from the Eucharist, causing uproar among the members.

This was certainly achieved by the US Catholic bishops with President Richard Nixon. In 1969 Nixon accepted that family planning was critical to the world's wellbeing and said in a message to Congress:

> *"When future generations evaluate the record of our time, one of the most important factors in their judgment will be the way*

in which we respond to population growth. Let us act in such a way that those who come after us - even as they lift their eyes beyond Earth's bounds - can do so with pride in the planet on which they live, with gratitude to those who lived on it in the past, and with continuing confidence in the future."

It was a remarkable statement but anathema to the bishops, and within five years the Administration was in full retreat.

In 1970 Nixon had created the Commission on Population Growth and the American Future, which after two years of study made more than 70 recommendations. They included making contraception and safe abortion available for all who needed them, if necessary at governments' expense. However, 1972 was a presidential election year and Nixon became convinced that the Catholic bishops would be able to swing the balance of voting against him. He completely abandoned the report even though he had himself commissioned it, and none of the recommendations was ever adopted. In 1974 he had another try, ordering all agencies of the federal government through National Security Study Memorandum 200 (NSSM 200) to determine the "implications of world population growth". However, by the time it reported in 1975 he had been forced to resign and was succeeded by President Ford, who made sure it went nowhere.

The report concluded that continued rapid population growth posed a risk to:

"world economic, political, and ecological systems and, as these systems begin to fail, to our humanitarian values".

It also stated that:

"population factors are indeed critical in, and often determinants of, violent conflict in developing areas,"

including both civil wars and regional conflicts. They could weaken unstable governments and "open the way to extremist regimes". It recommended:

"developing countries make family planning information, education and means available to all their peoples by 1980,"

with the United States contributing financially and offering medical and technical support. Again the Catholic bishops mobilised against it, adopting a plan to build a coalition against these proposals which involved the extreme right across the country. The NSSM 200 report, although endorsed by President Ford, was never published and, astonishingly, it became a classified document – although it was predictably leaked out. Under President Reagan, whose top team included a high proportion of conservative Catholics, the Administration agreed to alter its foreign aid programme to incorporate an outright "global gag" ban on the use of its aid funds if they included any help for birth control or abortion. Officials of the US Agency for International Development (AID) were sent to Rome for long discussions with the Holy See, and were finally obliged to reverse many of their programmes, or forced to resign. All funding was cut off for the International Planned Parenthood Federation (IPPF) and UN Fund for Population. During the Bush years, and later under Trump, funding was also withheld for the UN Children's Fund (Unicef) to help street children and families in extreme poverty.

This in turn has had a profoundly inhibiting effect on the United Nations, its agencies and the international development scene. Other countries, especially in Europe, have made up some of the shortfall in funding from the US, but until recently were unable to match the amounts involved.

Even under President Obama, although some funding was restored the commitment to family planning was still less than previous levels. The Trump administration, with its loyal supporters in the evangelical fundamentalist groups as well as the Catholic bishops, needed no encouragement to block family planning where it could, under the "pro-life" flag which was supposed to stop abortions but blocked contraception as well, leading to more unplanned pregnancies and more abortions. The move also included diversion of aid money to groups which were spreading false information about family planning and advocating abstinence from sex – which also increased the prevalence of unprotected sex. It was not until the new President Joe Biden, a liberal and pro-choice Catholic, entered the White House that new efforts were made to restore funding.

Disposable women

Although the overall pattern of Holy See/ Vatican activity has been ultra-conservative there was a period, while there were debates around the Pontifical Commission on Birth Control and the 1968 *Humanae Vitae* edict, when the Holy See looked as if it might take a more charitable view. I was at an international development conference in 1970 where there was a delightful Holy See representative whose favourite expression was "Down with the Pill!" Certainly no such jokes would be allowed now. The ultra-conservatives are firmly in charge of the Catholic hierarchy, and particularly its international operations. Their most recent tactic is to establish a coalition of ultra-conservative elements - including fundamentalists of other religions - against women's rights.

The Islamic world has been well aware of the anomalous position of the Holy See/ Vatican, and wanted a piece of the action for themselves. The UN, if it was not prepared to challenge the Holy See claims, could hardly refuse this new demand. The result is the Permanent Delegation of the Organisation of Islamic Cooperation (OIC) to the UN Offices in Geneva and Paris. Since there is no single body representing all Muslims this is something cobbled together for international representation. It was always likely to pursue only the most conservative version of an Islamic view of the world, and one which wholly or largely excludes women's views. It has much less access to international debates than the Holy See/ Vatican, but this move does mean getting a foot on the international ladder. It is heavily funded by conservative governments and wealthy individuals in Islamic countries, and their UN presence now means they can more easily co-ordinate the governments of Islamic-majority countries to speak and vote against measures they oppose. Other conservative and fundamentalist religious groups might make similar demands for representation at the UN and its development agencies, and if this happens it will further strengthen the fundamentalist bloc, organising largely to oppose family planning.

The OIC has already joined forces with the Holy See at specialised UN conferences to oppose family planning and sexual health generally. At the 2012 "Rio+20" Earth Summit on sustainable development, for example, all reference to "reproductive rights" was rigorously excluded from the final text, and no recognition of the link between family planning and international development was allowed into the document. The notion of women's rights generally was also excluded, despite the advocacy of women's and family planning organisations. They were overcome by a small minority of implacable opponents among the government delegations, organised by the Holy See, and including the representatives of the Philippines, Argentina, Malta and Egypt. In that same year a proposed UN declaration on the rights of women, including an end to domestic violence and marital rape, was opposed by delegations from the Holy See, Russia, Pakistan, Iran and Syria. At that time Egypt was governed by the Muslim Brotherhood, which claimed that the declaration would lead to the "complete disintegration of society".

"Flexing its political muscles"

The case of Russia opposing women's rights seems anomalous, but it is consistent with its support and even finance for ultra-conservative groups in other countries, including the Front Populaire in France, the Trump election campaign in the US, and the Brexit campaign in the UK. One commentator observed:

> *"Russia is simply trying to flex its political muscle in the international sphere to show that it is a force to be reckoned with".*

In other words there is an element of mischief here, an anti-democracy stance which uses the ultra-conservatives in the West as its chosen instrument. It is a revival of the old Communist International (Comintern) methods perhaps, but now using and reinforcing the right-wingers.

Russian internet actors are among those actively promoting "anti-vax" (anti-vaccination) campaigns in western countries, probably as a means of spreading doubt and distrust in scientific experts and health authorities, and to destabilise democratically elected governments. Bill Gates of Microsoft is a particular target for abuse, with various wild conspiracy theories such as the idea that he is implanting microchips with the Covid-19 vaccine to monitor people's actions. This has also increased vaccine hesitancy which is reducing the uptake of anti-Covid vaccines. It is no coincidence, I suggest, that the big contributions by Bill and Melinda Gates to family planning efforts, including FP2020 and FP2030, are unwelcome to the "pro-lifers" who also spread disinformation as an essential part of their campaigns. Melinda Gates, incidentally, is a committed Catholic who supports family planning.

The Russian Orthodox Church is also increasingly influential inside Russia and the Orthodox leadership has been opposing women's rights, even protection from domestic violence, while also condemning contraception and abortion. The Orthodox Church leader, Patriarch Kirill, met the Catholic Pope for the first time in 2016 and may have been influenced by him: he has even claimed that "feminism could destroy Russia"

On the international scene the Russian Government's influence has also tended to silence some countries which otherwise promote women's rights, including Cuba and Ecuador, because they see Russia as a key political ally. In the otherwise progressive European block of countries, Poland, Malta and Hungary - all with ultra-conservative governments - have also reversed their previous support for women's rights. Women, and women's rights, are becoming disposable, a bargaining chip within national and international politics. If a government has domestic problems with religious fundamentalists then cheap concessions can be made in the international forums on women and especially access to contraception, in the hope of securing the conservatives' political support at home.

Women out in the cold

In recent UN conferences some delegates have been observed following the Holy See's line against women's rights, following heavy personal lobbying, even though it contradicted the policies pursued by their own governments. Many smaller countries do not have sophisticated systems for briefing their delegates and issuing instructions, and their capabilities are also a small fraction of the assets and personnel controlled by the Holy See and other conservative forces.

Their delegates may be able to revert to their own personal prejudices, or persuaded by conservative lobbyists and delegations to follow their line, especially on issues of "culture" and women. Delegates are also subject to influence by the right-wing American groups which have set up lavishly funded events aimed at them while they are at the meetings.

Margaret Owen, a veteran of UN meetings who represents widows internationally, summed up the deteriorating situation at these meetings in a 2013 report on the Commission on the Status of Women:

> *"States are now regrouping in problematic combinations - for women's reproductive rights - to show their strength and muscle."*

She particularly cited disappointment that the delegation from Bangladesh:

> *"that led, for years in the South Asia region, on family plan-*
> *ning services and programmes, that targeted hard-to-reach*
> *women, should have now wandered to the other side."*

She paints a picture of closeted delegates making their decisions in the main building while six women from non-governmental organisations were

> *"talking mostly to each other in the 'ghetto' of the Church*
> *Centre, that lies across the road from the UN building,"*

discussing many other topics like torture and rape, genital mutilation, criminal trafficking, acid attacks and murder. With limited access to observer passes, and no speaking rights, many had been excluded from the UN building itself. Meanwhile the Holy See delegation has full access and is able to use complex manoeuvres and heavy lobbying of conservatives of other delegations inside and outside the building, not only to block new rights for women but even, wherever possible, to weaken the texts previously.

There seems to be an element of apathy creeping into the debates. One initiative after another for women's rights, against sexual violence, for homosexual rights and especially for reproductive rights is being blocked and even pushed back by these growing alliances of ultra-conservatives, led by the Holy See. There can be a strong feeling among some non-governmental organisations that the battles are just not worth it - or that the only people who can fight them are a handful of mainly western developed countries which keep pressing for a rights agenda. They are rights that can so easily be blocked by a single opponent, and now by the growing alliances of the Catholic bishops, Islamists and ultra-conservatives even from countries whose own policies are solid. During the Trump years there were also evangelical fundamentalists running US policy which was closely aligned with that group.

The result of all these processes is that, despite conference after conference on women's rights, reproductive rights and sustainable development, the UN system and its specialised agencies are still having to base their actions on the 1994 Cairo Conference on Population and Development (ICPD). Where there have been bold declarations in favour of family planning, as with the first Regional Conference on Population and Development for Latin America and the Caribbean in 2013, the negotiations were led mostly by experts (whether from Ministries of Women or Health) rather than by the Ministries of Foreign Affairs which continue to dominate most of the UN meetings and which are not in touch with the real issues on the ground.

The one major achievement recently has been the incorporation of family planning into the Sustainable Development Goals of 2015, a triumph which reversed the Holy See's successful blocking of this element from the previous Millennium Development Goals of 2001. Goal 3.7 of the new SDGs reads:

> *"By 2030, ensure universal access to sexual and reproductive health-care services, including for family planning, information and education, and the integration of reproductive health into national strategies and programmes."*

Goal 5.6 reads:

> *"Ensure universal access to sexual and reproductive health and reproductive rights."*

These clauses were achieved with an almost superhuman effort by governments and non-governmental organisations. One battle won: so many more to go.

As long as the agenda for family planning is set in terms of human rights and especially women's rights, I suggest, it will be an uphill battle in the international conferences which determine principles and policies. This is why, in the next chapter, I suggest that we abandon cherished positions which are not opening up the debate, and rethink our tactics.

Resources

Catholics for Choice, *The Catholic Church at the United Nations: Church or State?,* Washington DC, 2013. ISBN: 978-1-936421-05-3. Catholics for Choice have a "See Change" campaign to challenge the Holy See's representation at the UN.

Stephen D Mumford, "The Vatican's Role in the World Population Crisis: the untold story," presentation to Main Line Unitarian Church, 1996 (Center for Research on Population and Security, 1996).

Michelle Goldberg, *The Means of Reproduction: Sex, Power and the Future of the World* (Penguin Press, New York, 2009).

Derek S Hoff, *The State and the Stork: The population debate and policy making in US history* (University of Chicago Press, 2012).

Stephen D Mumford, *The Life and Death of NSSM 200: How the destruction of political will doomed a U.S. population policy*, (Amazon.com, 1996).

Carl Bernstein, "The US and the Vatican on Birth Control,"*Time* magazine, 24 February 1992.

PART FOUR

SOLUTIONS

Chapter eight

A NEW WAY FORWARD: BASIC NEEDS

In the richer countries modern contraception, now almost universal, has benefitted everybody either directly or indirectly. Good family planning is one important though often overlooked reason these countries have become so much richer than the rest of the world. Over the last century contraception and improved maternity care have enormously improved women's and children's health and survival prospects, causing death rates to come down with astonishing speed. Formal education is now provided for every child, and many go on to higher education and levels of expertise especially in science, technology and engineering that have fuelled their country's wealth creation.

This is a surprisingly recent development: it is only two or three generations ago that women were forced to bear children they did not want, where many were injured or died in childbirth or from illegal and dangerous abortions, and where infant mortality was a fact of life. There are people still living in these wealthier countries who were born into a world of very large families of ten or more surviving children, often growing up in poverty. Two of my grandparents were born into these big families. At that time the only answer to the "surplus" population as the children grew up was to encourage emigration to every other continent in the world – often imposing settler populations by force – with all the long-term disruption and conflict that resulted and which still persists in the world today.

Family planning in the wealthier countries has now been embedded in health services, and in many it is free of charge. This now means that the numbers of children in each family are now largely in line with what parents want and can support. Women were freed from the struggle to feed and clothe all those unplanned children and have entered higher education and jobs in very large numbers. We have now become an integral part of the workplace, contributing to household and national income and gaining personal autonomy and a large degree of equality with men. Nobody would claim there are no problems left for women in these countries, but the progress in terms of health and welfare (and contribution to GDP) has been astonishing.

This also means that most countries of Europe, North America and Australasia have generally stable population numbers. Although distorted by birth "bulges" especially after World War 2, the population is also on the way to becoming balanced between different age groups. The main source of any population growth in the West now is immigration and longer life expectancy, not births. If the worst that people there can find to worry about is our better health and attractiveness to migrants from poorer and conflict-ridden countries with growing numbers, then we have come a long way.

This is now perhaps the biggest difference between rich and poor countries: we have modern contraception and they on the whole (with some notable exceptions) do not, or only for the privileged few. On the international scene double standards rule: the idea that modern contraception is not relevant or even dangerous for "them" but not for "us". Some are even claiming that providing family planning is a cultural imposition for "them" but not for "us". It is a case of international double standards.

The same basic human needs should be recognized everywhere. We should extend services to meet those needs in the poorer countries and the poorest people within them, so that the benefits that have contributed so much to western health, welfare and development can be available to all. While this is not the only anti-poverty measure that is necessary, it is crucially important and can have a multiplier effect in, for example, enabling the extension of education to a higher proportion of the children. We should not tolerate the gulf between richer countries, where people can make critical life decisions about pregnancy and children, and poorer ones where they do not have the means to make these decisions but can too easily be overwhelmed by random life events such as illness, loss of income or extra mouths to feed.

Sidestepping the opposition

If we are to move get worldwide access to the choices now enjoyed mainly by the wealthier countries and people, I am suggesting abandoning the attachment of the population organisations to "sexual and reproductive health and rights" or "SRHR". As we have seen in the last chapter, the reproductive rights case has been repeatedly beaten back by the Catholic hierarchy together with fundamentalists and nationalists in different countries. Their growing alliance means that they can prevent "SRHR" from becoming a universally accepted mainstream agenda. The Holy See/ Vatican, alongside ultra-conservative and autocratic governments in the Islamic world and elsewhere, have built an increasing resistance in international meetings to any progress on women's rights or even human rights generally. They are carrying out a military-style "search and destroy" operation on any mention or hint of women's rights that might suggest the right to make our own decisions about children. Even if Pope Francis were able to reduce the Vatican's ferocity and funding on this, which looks unlikely, the opposition is now entrenched. We should be realistic: the reaction against family planning as an element in women's rights is so strong that we need to sidestep it with a new agenda of our own.

If they use their strongest tactics, so should we. Although human rights are central to the international agenda, and so is family planning, attaching the two together is a dead end. Our side has won important battles without the SRHR label, like incorporating reproductive choice into the recent Sustainable Development Goals. There will be a constant battle to ensure that this is funded on the scale that is required to meet the needs, since other SDGs may get most of the money and the effort if there is not constant vigilance. We do not need to handicap our efforts with our favourite obscure initials. Language matters, as any Holy See representative would tell you (if they were willing to have an honest conversation about their tactics).

The case for arguing needs instead of rights – especially for women and children – is that basic needs are universal. Rights (whether we like it or not) can be subject to different cultural and legal environments, and a push-back from those who benefit from the current situation. Despite the enormous international efforts to achieve a universal standard of human rights worldwide, especially over the last 70 years, these are under constant challenge from reactionaries. The battle for women's rights as an integral element of that must also go on. But the millions of women who face insurmountable barriers to choices should not have to wait for that particular fight to be won.

The case for people being able to choose the numbers and timing of children should be pursued separately, and as a matter of urgency. We must support the choices that will help people move out of the vicious circle of poverty, hunger and illness. The UN calculates that 36 million die of hunger and malnutrition every year: one person every second, most of them women and children. Unintended births contribute to this horror, unacceptable in a world which is trying to end poverty, fight illness and promote inclusion.

Safeguarding rights while meeting needs

I suggest too that it would also be better for the universal human rights agenda if family planning is dealt with separately. The fight for human rights must go on, of course – the right to life, to freedom from torture or slavery and the right to family life. Women's rights in general – against rape and domestic violence, against genital mutilation, against rape or forced marriage, against trafficking and exploitation – also need to be an integral part of the universal human rights agenda, which until recently they have not been. Separating sexual health from the rights agenda could be critical to success: advancing women's right to equal treatment under law, the right to own property, to equal rights at work, to freedom from forced marriage and rape, to keeping their children if the marriage fails, freedom from discrimination, the right to education and the vote, freedom of movement and the right to life itself.

The term "Sexual and Reproductive Health and Rights" confronts further resistance from the opposition because of the reference to sexuality. Not only is women's sexuality a forbidden topic for many conservative societies and governments, but the SRHR banner has also been extended by its advocates to incorporate the rights of lesbians and gay men, bisexuals, transsexuals, questioning and intersex. That agenda is also very important, but it should be tackled separately and not as an add-on to SRHR. Otherwise the anti-gay backlash starts to overlap with the anti-choice one, and a proper discussion becomes obscured and overlaid with the sometimes hysterical reaction from some conservatives to either or both.

As for the family planning advocates, it is time to find new ways forward that are based on goals which are universally supported: reducing poverty, promoting development, improving health. We have been locked into a trying to be an irresistible progressive force (us) confronted by an immoveable reactionary object (them) and the result is that we have been bashing our collective heads against a brick wall of refusal that is simply being built higher and higher. We need more sophisticated tactics which would mean we sidestep that wall, making their arguments about religious dogmas or "culture" as irrelevant as the medieval disputes within the Catholic Church about how many angels could stand on the head of a pin. How would it look if the religious started opposing motions for saving lives, relieving poverty and promoting individual and family health and welfare? We should think tactically, choose our battles, abandon the battles of "rights" versus "culture" and call for meeting the needs of all people everywhere.

A hierarchy of needs?

If we want to gain momentum on choices we should be embedding our case into the drive against poverty and speaking the language of basic needs. There is a universal human need for food and water to sustain life, the health and welfare of children and families, and stable families and communities to ensure our health and wellbeing. The issue of human needs is a complex one, and we have to work out how best to define this for women.

Abraham Maslow first introduced his concept of basic needs, and a hierarchy of needs, in his 1943 paper "A Theory of Human Motivation". This hierarchy suggests that people are motivated to fulfil basic needs before moving on to other, more advanced needs. He suggested that people have an inborn desire to be self-actualized, that is, to be all they can be. In order to achieve these ultimate goals, however, a number of more basic needs must be met such as the need for food, safety, love, and self-esteem.

The most basic needs, he suggests, are physiological: food, water, air to breathe, and homeostasis (a state of health which is maintained by the constant adjustment of biochemical and physiological pathways) He also included a liveable temperature, clothing and shelter.

The next level of needs would be safety and security: individual freedom from violent assault or coercion, collective protection from external or internal threats to the community, freedom from fear, and financial stability.

Physical and safety needs, Maslow suggests, make up people's basic needs. Beyond that there are social needs, including for love and a sense of belonging to family or community, together with "esteem" needs, which means feeling respected and valued. At the top of his hierarchy of needs is "self-actualisation", meaning the full use and exploitation of talents and capabilities. Maslow's own summary is:

"What a man can be, he must be."

This of course gives away the obvious point that his approach is focused on men and not women. The theory has also been criticized in terms of his proposed hierarchy, which would not be universally accepted – for example, the need to belong to their family or community might be even more important for many people than some of the physical needs. While there is much debate about his proposals about a hierarchy of needs they have been massively influential, feeding into the idea of universal basic needs which is at the heart of agreed international development objectives.

There is now scope for much more discussion of whether and how Maslow's and other male-focused approaches can be revised to relate to girls' and women's needs. I suggest that before even the need for food and drink is the importance of bodily integrity or of survival itself. The threat or use of violence, including rape and assault both in the home and outside, threaten a woman's very life. Forced marriage and sex, especially if imposed on children, undermine a girl's or woman's identity and sense of herself as an individual. Within a husband's family she can be made into his possession and often the unpaid servant of his whole family. If she is left with no family her only means of survival may be to enter the huge sex work industry, with all its cruelties and abuses.

Freedom from life-threatening coercion and the fear of coercion seem to me to be even more fundamental to women and girls than food and drink. Where her life is at risk because of the pressure to get pregnant and have a baby, and the threat of violence or rejection by the family if she resists, the ability to make her own life choices could mean the difference between life and death. In abusive situations girls and women live with constant fear. There are of course further issues of survival in the practice of female genital mutilation, a form of extreme torture used on girls which also threatens the health and even the life of the victim.

Overall, safety and security are on the same level as food and drink for women. In some situations of extreme threat they may even be seen as the most basic need there could possibly be. So many women are unable to attain even the most basic health and welfare in a system which also imposes pregnancy and the choice of either a dangerous abortion or enforced childbirth. I would argue that the ability to choose to get pregnant and have a baby is one of the basic needs for girls and women who are living in poverty.

Needs in this matter are expressed quite differently by women in richer and poorer situations. An interesting contribution is by the Irish obstetrician Mary Higgins, who stresses the different needs of women facing childbirth, depending on the level of medical support they can expect:

> *"At any time nature can bring a woman right down the hierarchy of needs to the fundamentals: pregnant women facing homelessness, women and partners newly unemployed, an abruption, an intrauterine death, an eclamptic fit. Our focus in the developed world is now on bringing the balance back from too much medical care rather than worrying about too little, but the fulcrum swings differently elsewhere. It is an aspiration that women and families in other countries can have these fundamental needs met, so that they can concentrate on self-actualisation while having the full safety net of medical care."*

New priorities

If we are to provide for women's basic needs we should also stress children's basic need for health and nutrition, and to be brought up in stable families and communities. This would mean no more abandoned children, no more dead babies on rubbish heaps, no children trying to survive in the street because they have no home, no more children available to child traffickers, sex abusers and enslavers.

We should not forget either the needs of our natural environment if we are to live well: fresh water, viable agricultural land and fisheries, and an ecological balance with forests, grasslands and seas. We must be aware of the increasing conflicts over water resources, whether local or national, which increasing numbers of people bring. Many women and children are forced to spend hours carrying heavy loads of water for their families, sometimes over long distances, taking many hours every day. The climate crisis is increasing the difficulty of finding clean water, cultivating the soil and keeping livestock.

Poverty means a lack of security, where unexpected life events like illness, unemployment or deaths can lead to serious problems that would not arise if the family had some money. An unexpected, unwanted pregnancy can often tip the balance between survival and disaster. Family resources which are enough to meet the basic needs for the life and health of all its members may become inadequate if there are any more children. Even worse is the loss or ill-health of a mother, which is happening with deadly regularity and is a tragedy for people in many poor communities.

Children without a mother may find that they end up starving, homeless and with the most dismal future. Their best hope in many cases is to be brought into the family of their mother's sister, grandmother or other relative, although those may already be struggling to provide enough food for their existing children. By sharing it out more thinly this will mean all the children have too little to eat, let alone education or the prospect of a livelihood when they grow up. This is obvious to women everywhere, which is why such enormous numbers of women go for illegal abortions despite knowing just how dangerous they are and that they could even die as a result.

There are certain categories of women with an even greater need for the security provided by family planning. Most obvious of these are the very young women and girls who are already having sex but their bodies are too immature to bear children safely, or their circumstances mean that they would be forced out of education or a job, or thrown out of their own families, if they become pregnant. Millions of girls and young women are facing unwanted pregnancy through forced marriage, from sexual violence, or through the "sugar daddy" system of sex with an older and wealthier man.

Women building up a livelihood, whether as employees or as independent farmers or traders, may need a period without pregnancy in order to establish themselves. Those who already have one or more children may need a respite from pregnancy to allow their bodies to recover fully, and to feed and care for their existing children. Those who are sick or malnourished may also need relief from the heavy demands of pregnancy. Women approaching the menopause may need the assurance that they will not have yet another child if they do not want that, if the family would suffer or if their health would be badly affected. Sometimes women need help to conceive when they want to, or to carry a pregnancy to term: real choices about children would mean support for their needs as well.

Pressing for women's basic needs could transform the debate about population and family planning. We should be arguing that women's basic needs are the same, everywhere.

"Do we not bleed?"

Need is a powerful notion.. A core element in any development process should be people's need to make their own life decisions. This need for family planning focuses on women because we bear the children but it also applies to men, since their interests in stable families are just as important though perhaps less obvious. Marriage and relationships are often far from perfect, but for many men their wife is precious and irreplaceable. How sad it is when they see this only after she dies, perhaps in childbirth. Yet the biggest need of all belongs with the women themselves, and of course the children. All women need their health and strength not only for themselves, but in order to look after children and often other dependants – older or disabled – who may have nobody else to care for and support them.

This is the missing link in so many poverty eradication strategies. Nobody should pretend that family planning alone will solve all the problems of poverty (our opponents love to claim that we say it will). Without it, though, the battle will always be uphill, a never-ending struggle to contend with the downward forces of enforced sex and marriage for women, enforced pregnancies, and more children than they can safely bear or are able to feed and care for.

It is the needs of individuals – women, men and children – that should always come first in this debate. Too often we hear both theorists and practitioners of development talk about "population" only as a way to address the growth in human numbers. Although we cannot avoid the use of the population concept, it is an argument that is going nowhere. It has become that unwanted old, smelly dog, a toxic P-word in many international circles.

"Population" is also addressing the issue from completely the wrong direction. We should not be advocating choice merely because the abstract concept of "population" demands it. We should be pressing for individual welfare and development through a greater ability to make life decisions. Individual and family needs should always be the focus if poverty itself is to be overcome. Look after the people, and the population will take care of itself.

Cultures, governments and laws differ around the world, but human bodies remain the same everywhere. We need enough food of good nutritional value, water and good enough health, wherever we are. Our capacity for reproduction is the same world-wide, and our need to control that is universal. Women's particular needs around sex, pregnancy, childbearing and child rearing are the same in any part of the world.

I am reminded of the famous speech by Shakespeare's Shylock in *The Merchant of Venice*, raging at his treatment as a Jew. Changing the text slightly:

> *"I am a poor woman. Has not any woman eyes? Has not any woman hands, organs, dimensions, senses, affections, passions? Fed with the same food, hurt with the same weapons, subject to the same diseases, healed by the same means... If you prick us, do we not bleed? If you tickle us, do we not laugh? If you poison us, do we not die?"*

Everybody's needs can be met if there are enough resources (water, food, housing, health care) and no discrimination in how they are distributed. The question of hugely unequal resources which underlies all development applies very much to choosing children: the more developed a country is, the more likely its people are to have that choice. The poorer it is – with a few notable exceptions – the less likely to have any choice. Within each country, too, it is the poorest women who have the least choice, and with that the greatest risk of unwanted pregnancies, dangerous abortions, and a serious risk of death or serious disability for themselves and for their children. Family planning is essential to any moves to combat poverty.

Resources

Michelle Goldberg, *The Means of Reproduction: Sex, Power, and the Future of the World* (Penguin Press, New York, 2009).

Abraham Maslow, "A Theory of Human Motivation" (paper, 1943), followed by *Motivation and Personality* (Harper, 1954).

Mary Higgins "Maslow and maternity care—how to reconcile experiences that are poles apart?" *British Medical Journal*, 2 June 2017.

Chapter nine

SEX, HEALTH AND CHOICES

I once came across a booklet with the title "Sex and Local Radio". You had to read the whole thing to see the joke: there was no mention of sex in the book, but you had already read it. This is not one of those since sex is what this is all about.

Sex is popular everywhere, but especially in poor communities where it is perhaps the only entertainment that costs nothing. Where women get their own pleasure from sex, that is the ideal. But we should also recognise that far too often, sex is an obligation that men can impose on women. It is important to be realistic about sex, especially in repressive relationships and societies. Here girls and women have little or no choice in the matter if the law does not allow them to choose their partners or refuse sex. Marital rape is not a crime, domestic violence and abuse are accepted as normal, and many religious authorities order wives to allow their husbands to have sex at any time. Many of the religious moralisers who are so quick to condemn any women who step out of line are very unwilling to enforce any morality on the men.

These moralisers are often in favour of sexual co-ercion since, to be frank, some of them get their own sexual gratification in this way. It could even be one of the perks of the job. They may also see sexual freedom for all the men as a means to producing more and more children to boost their own status. They are very quiet about telling other men to refrain from sexual violence or from forcing girls and women into marriage or sex. If priests, imams and all the rest were to preach a genuine sexual morality for men as well as women we would have much less violence, better relationships and many fewer unwanted pregnancies and births. If condemnation is to be reserved for women only you have to wonder whose religion this is, and whether their God really approves of the men hijacking the religion in their own interest. The leaders' sometimes obsessive attention is often directed at controlling women, instructing them how to do it, when to do it, with whom, and damn the consequences.

In the real world sexuality is infinitely variable, subject to a complex variety of emotions, and quite often without thought for the consequences. Good sex, freely chosen, is better when there is no worry about unwanted pregnancy. Routine "good enough" sex needs contraception. Sex as an obligation or a business transaction, through rape, coercion or forced marriage, means women are in even greater need of it to preserve some element of control over their own bodies. This is all too prevalent in poorer communities. As the Ugandan doctor Lydia Mungherera told Michelle Goldberg:

> "Women don't have rights in deciding when to have sex, and how to have sex - whether to use a condom or not. Men can have as many partners as they want, and women don't have a

> *choice. You find that women are locked up in marriages where they're not happy, and they don't have the financial and educational empowerment to leave those marriages. There's a lot of domestic violence."*

If we could be more realistic about what sex is really like for millions of women we could perhaps see that they have an even greater need for protection from unwanted pregnancy than those women who are able to decide when to have sex, and who their partner will be.

Women's secret knowledge

It is too often claimed that women will not adopt family planning until they have been to school, and this has become a tired cliché of development thinking. It is true of course that there is a correlation: women with education are likely to move out of the poorest category and have more choices, more money as well as knowledge of what is available and where. However it is not true that poor women with little or no formal education will not want contraception. There are now many projects demonstrating this to be a patronising view of poor women, who are just as keen to make their own decisions about pregnancy as those with more money and education once they have the information and the access. Many women walk long distances, using time and energy they can hardly afford, to get their supplies of contraception. This has nothing to do with their education and everything to do with what they need.

A feature of many poor areas is that the women there have lost many of the traditional methods of limiting pregnancies. These may include women's secret societies and rituals, including the initiation of young girls; sometimes the physical separation of new mothers and babies; extended periods of breast-feeding; and contraception and abortion with the use of techniques and especially medicinal herbs known to "wise women" in the community. Modern societies have tended to overlook and devalue women's knowledge and skills and suppress women's autonomy and ability to organise and teach the younger ones, sometimes through initiation, with the knowledge passed on including traditional forms of birth control.

In Europe and the newly settled United States, in previous centuries, women with this knowledge and skills were branded as "witches", and many were tortured and killed. The result was to intensify the cruelties involved in denying women choices about children, including the neglect or killing of unwanted babies - especially if they were girls or born with disabilities. Modern medicine and science allow us all to move past these horrors and regulate births in safer and more effective ways. It offers a shift towards a more humane tradition.

The process of modernisation or westernisation which is contained within "development" has, since colonial times, reduced the power and influence of women in traditional societies, as I argue in *The Domestication of Women*. This has often meant that the women started losing their own ways of doing things, and made to accept the men's version of what "our tradition" is about. It is often claimed by men, including in international forums, that "our tradition" demands large numbers of babies. But cultures are dynamic, and changing rapidly with "development". They depend on different perspectives within the community, and especially between old and young, women and men. Let the women and men together decide what is right for them and their communities, and find a balance of old and new traditions which is healthy for everyone.

Writing as a woman in a developed country, where there have been rapid changes in what is available, I have relied on contraception to enable good health and a life I have decided for myself, within or outside relationships. It has enabled me to choose the right number of children for me (in my case, none) which I hope is of benefit to society. I want that possibility to be available to all women everywhere, no matter what their personal circumstances or obligations. We now have the means to offer contraception and early abortion which is safe and effective, in any area of any country in the world: something that has never existed before. All we need are the resources.

Can do

The list of governments which have understood and promoted birth control options for their people is surprising. One of the poorest countries in the world, Bangladesh, has instituted wide-ranging programmes, with the support of international agencies and voluntary aid groups. One of the countries most recently torn by civil conflict, Rwanda, has done the same. One of the most strictly Islamic, Iran, has made it a high priority with great success, although it is now starting to retreat. Poverty and conflict do not prevent enlightened thinking by governments. They can be the reason it becomes a high priority. Yet many other governments around the world still use underdevelopment and poverty as an excuse to do nothing. "More children, and yet more!" is their mantra. It is numbers they want, not better lives - quantity and not quality of life - and they will use "our culture" as an excuse.

The numbers are for cannon fodder, for cheap labour and child labour, for perceived advantage in sectarian conflicts, and as members of their religious or ethnic group in competition with others. They may also see increasing numbers as the key to winning elections to keep them comfortably in power - sometimes to use the resources of the state to enrich themselves, their own families and their supporters. They then wonder why there is so much poverty, so many homeless children, youth unemployment, crime, mass migrations, environmental destruction and burning of wild areas, warlords and terrorist groups, and vicious armed conflicts.

Governments and the international community are unanimous in wanting economic development. They also, of course, want peace and stability. Yet this cannot happen while so many people are subject to life events - births, deaths, illness and disability, debt and dependency, loss of land or animals, environmental disasters, sectarian conflicts and crime - with no possibility of deciding whether or when to have more children in that situation. An unwanted pregnancy can be the disaster that pushes whole families into deep poverty, and a dangerous abortion may then be their only way of trying to avert that disaster. To have any chance at all of improving their lives, and their health and welfare, people living in poverty need to be able to make these crucial life decisions for themselves. In many areas where there is no modern family planning provision at all, people do not even believe it is possible. It is only when there is a safe and effective programme that they will gain the confidence that will enable them to take control. We are not talking about the impossible. It has been estimated that if half of all women had one less child, population growth would stop and our numbers would be stable.

"Devastating"

Governments hold the key to effective action, whether the donors giving more money or recipients giving higher priority to this in their policies. The international effort to bring modern contraception is long on experience and expertise, but very short on finance. Programmes are at crisis point, with some donor governments pulling out the rug from under critical work. The only UN agency offering any funds is the UN Fund for Population (UNFPA) which has very limited resources. It is worth noting that the "Brexit" vote in Britain was considered a serious blow to international contraceptive programmes. The reason? Britain has been one of the biggest supporters, through its international aid, and the fall in the pound following that vote meant 10% less money in dollars for family planning. In 2021 the same government suddenly announced that as part of major cuts in overseas aid it would slash 85% of its agreed contributions to UNFPA Supplies, and a $17 million cut to core operating funds. This was especially damaging because the UK had always been a leading funder of family planning. In a carefully considered statement the Executive Director of UNFPA said:

> *These cuts will be devastating for women and girls and their families across the world… [they] would have helped prevent*

around 250,000 maternal and child deaths, 14.6 million
unintended pregnancies and 4.3 million unsafe abortions."

With Trump in power in the US, there were savage cuts to family planning programmes, a "global gag" and certainly little or no increase in international funds for family planning. The only way forward at that point was for private sector funders such as the Gates Foundation to put money into new services, but it was like trying to stop a retreat rather being able to make a decisive move forward.

The scale of the shortfall demands governmental and international action and greatly increased funds. With a new Biden Administration in the United States, the damage done by Trump and the US pro-natalists in withdrawing from international co-operation on this is being stopped, and reversed. We have finally said goodbye to the "global gag rule" (GGR) which required non-governmental organisations to certify that they would not "perform or actively promote abortion as a method of family planning" as a condition of receiving US Government family planning assistance. It has been estimated by the Guttmacher Institute that under the Trump administration the gag was applied to almost $12 billion in funding. Many leading family planning organisations had to continue with reduced budgets and contracting services because they refused to accept the GGR prohibitions. It also harmed other health programmes, especially those limiting the spread of HIV/ AIDS. Last but not least, by cutting the provision of contraception it also increased the numbers of abortions.

While the US Administration has now changed hands, the "pro-lifers" will not be giving up the fight any time soon. The US Government's "Helms Amendment" was still prohibiting any US aid funds going directly to aid safer abortions. Battles over international assistance for family planning are sadly likely to continue for many years. Governments of the poorer countries need to start taking a lead themselves, putting this higher up their list of priorities for their own actions and for requests for international assistance. Support and expertise from the international community will be there if local and national governments in the poorer countries ask for it. Their representatives also need to take the initiative in international meetings to demand this support.

"She has already done her damage"

One of the causes of poverty - which is also a cause of great suffering - is the failure to ensure that all people have access to basic healthcare which is either free or at least at a cost they can afford. The luxury of health services that exist in wealthier countries is simply absent in most developing nations, especially among the poorest countries and the poorest of their people.

An estimated 150 million people each year are forced into poverty, or further into the deepest poverty and debt, because they have to pay high costs for medical treatment when there is illness or injury. If a family member dies there could well be funeral costs beyond what they can afford, which means getting heavily into debt. 400 million people do not have access to even the most basic health services. For many national governments, funding for health is just a very low priority. A recent report from the World Health Organization (WHO) shows that between 2000 and 2014, public funding for health from domestic sources in low and middle-income countries stagnated. The international target is now for all governments to spend 5% of their GDP on basic health care, with international donors supplementing this with carefully targeted interventions that supplement and, critically, do not replace national funding as has sometimes happened in the past.

A feature of development economics is the disregard for people's health as an element in transforming poverty into self-sufficiency. In cost-benefit analysis it gets very low or even zero recognition. Development economists are very much to blame here: they attach little or no monetary value to health, instead focusing on paid work and commercial outputs and also ignoring the huge amounts of unpaid work in any economy. They either have access to free health care or have health insurance to cover it. This means that they have a very superficial understanding of the importance of health care and of contraception in particular, something that they do not personally have to worry about, and this distorts their calculations.

The economists and planners find it surprising when the people in the area of a development project become hostile to them. If only they offered better health services for all as a routine element of a project they would have many fewer problems with this. They also need to lift their gaze from purely cost issues. I have heard one econ-omist, for example, claiming that it is not cost-effective to give contraception to a woman nearing the menopause because:

"she has already done her environmental damage".

That approach fails to take account of the influence of older women on younger people in deciding whether or not to use contraception. This kind of thinking is crude and offensive, a kind of colonial attitude which fails to recognise the needs of the people that development providers work with.

Voting for health

International organisations need to change their thinking, with health not only taking a higher priority but also incorporating family planning as an essential element. Ask the World Bank, IMF or UNDP about this and until now they would have little to say: they may merely suggest that health promotion and/ or family planning be added as an optional extra to major country investments.

      In many poor areas, if there is a medical service t specifically excludes family planning. Catholic clinics and hospitals are forbidden to offer any choices apart from complete abstinence from sex (as if that were possible) or the unreliable "rhythm method" of timed abstinence. I will argue that governments should consider taking over such health facilities as part of an official programme, which was done by the South African government as one of the first policy changes after the end of *apartheid*. Failing that, they should aim to offer a stand-alone family planning service with equal reach into the poorer communities, and they should insist that Catholic clinics and hospitals should refer their patients there as appropriate. It is not the most efficient approach, but it may be the only practical one. The same issues apply to the health services offered by some hard-line Islamist groups to poor people, in areas where there are no other medical services. These services provide a base for consolidating support for the extremists among the local community.

It is sad that most of the specialised agencies of the United Nations, including the World Health Organisation (WHO) and the UN Children's Fund (Unicef) are not providing reproductive health support as an integral part of their work. Their line, when questioned, is that this is the job only of the UN Fund for Population (UNFPA) who work alongside them in some areas. However, UNFPA's budget is very small compared to many of the other agencies, and it also has other activities such as census management which take some of the already limited funds. If real progress is to be made, all relevant agencies must incorporate choice about family size into their programmes, and their budgets.

International, national, local and non-governmental bodies should be challenged to accept reproductive health, alongside other health services, as a key element in any true development programme. It is very striking that many aid agencies have decided to exclude reproductive health and choices from their work. I have found that among British agencies, for example, Oxfam and Save the Children currently do little or nothing for reproductive health. An Oxfam representative defended their position by claiming that "others" will provide this service. In far too many areas in which they operate, that means no help at all. This needs to be reviewed as a matter of urgency.

Defending the services

Whenever a health emergency arises, family planning services are the first to be raided for resources, budgets and staff, because of their low profile politically. Basic health services are next on the list for a takeover. The coronavirus Covid-19 pandemic is no exception. Poonam Muttreja, Executive Director of the Population Foundation of India, commented in 2012:

> *"Tragically, disease outbreaks have always had a gendered impact, threatening women's access to health services. We have witnessed this in the past with Zika and Ebola epidemics… We must learn from past experiences and ensure that essential services like family planning are not compromised at the expense of health emergencies."*

In the Covid-19 pandemic it became very common for family planning services, staff and budgets to be raided to try and deal with the virus, whether through vaccinations or treatment. It is critically important that health and especially family planning become a higher priority for spending.

There are some encouraging signs of this happening. For example in 2016 there was a $500 million World Bank International Development Association credit to Nigeria for a "Saving One Million Lives" initiative for maternal and child health. The indicators for success here included contraceptive prevalence as well as maternal and child health and survival rates. This kind of programme needs to be rolled out to many more countries. The World Bank now has an important Global Financing Facility in Support of Every Woman, Every Child. While its title may be over-complicated, the international support for it has been very strong with financial contributions from many governments around the world. It is not often that the World Bank is ahead of the specialised agencies in humanitarian work, but this programme is proving that it can be.

There can be no real health or welfare without choice: spending on health and choice is an investment, not a cost. The UN's Global Strategy for Women's, Children's and Adolescents' Health (2016) showed that almost a quarter of income growth in low- and middle-income countries between 2000 and 2011 resulted from improved health outcomes. Until personal health is added into the development equation, with family planning as an essential element, any economic and social progress will be limited and limiting.

UHC = TLC (tender loving care)

With the worldwide Covid-19 pandemic, although it has devastated and overwhelmed many countries' health services, there is much greater international recognition of the crucial importance of healthcare, especially because of the damaging effects of lockdowns on national economies. This has given further impetus to the calls for "UHC", or Universal Health Care. This recognizes that people should:

> *"have access, without discrimination, to nationally determined sets of the needed promotive, preventive, curative, rehabilitative and palliative essential health services, and essential, safe, affordable, effective and quality medicines and vaccines, while ensuring that the use of these services does not expose the users to financial hardship, with a special emphasis on the poor, vulnerable and marginalized segments of the population."*

There are still battles going on about the inclusion of family planning within UHC. In 2019 there was a joint statement by the United States on behalf of Bahrain, Belarus, Brazil, Democratic Republic of the Congo, Egypt, Guatemala, Haiti, Hungary, Iraq, Libya, Mali, Nigeria, Poland, Russia, Saudi Arabia, Sudan, United Arab Emirates and Yemen::

> *"We do not support references to ambiguous terms and expressions, such as sexual and reproductive health and rights in UN documents, because they can undermine the critical role of the family and promote practices, like abortion, in circumstances that do not enjoy international consensus and which can be misinterpreted by UN agencies".*

With the US now shifting its position, that still leaves many of the countries on the list which have incorporated opposition to family planning into their policies, based on opposition to "rights" and especially "sexual rights". It underlines the importance of choice advocates shifting to the language of health needs, rather than an insistence on rights. "Need" is very much a part of the language of health.

The international campaigns for Universal Health Care have been met by campaigners working with the International Conference on Family Planning answering: "Not without fp". This could make it seem that we are against UHC if it excludes family planning, so a better formulation could be "including family planning". Whatever the slogans, the important message has to be: more universal health care, and more family planning. Preferably together, but if necessary as separate services.

A paper by Lynda Gilby and Meri Koivusalo summarises the importance of incorporating family planning services (SRH, or sexual and reproductive health) into universal health care, although they are still using the concept of "rights":

> *"Access to SRH services and the recognition of reproductive rights has been proven to lower the number of abortions, prevent unwanted pregnancies, reduce maternal deaths, and improve maternal and reproductive health. Therefore, inclusion of SRH*

services and the recognition of reproductive rights are a critical component of UHC."

There is no development without health, and no health without choices. So let us talk about health needs rather than rights. Women worldwide who need better health. Help us with this, and we can then fight for our rights.

Abortion as a fact of life

This would not be complete without discussing abortion as an essential element in family planning, a backup if contraception is unavailable or fails for some reason. At the moment the debate is between "pro-choice" and "pro-life" but the distinction is a false one: abortion is a fact of life and it is practically impossible to imagine a world without it. If there is no choice of legal and safe termination of pregnancy at an early stage, huge numbers of women resort to illegal and dangerous abortions which endanger their own lives.

Abortions are at epidemic levels in those countries which have made them illegal, too expensive or simply impossible to get. Hospital facilities which should be devoted to maternity and infant care struggle to cope with women suffering from the life-threatening emergencies and injuries caused by these abortions. This is even reported to be happening in richer countries like the United States where, although it is legal, persistent attacks on providers have closed many clinics so that it is just not available.

There is one slogan used by campaigners which is crucial to this:

"Keep it legal, keep it safe."

Nobody can stop abortion: it is universal and inevitable.

People have sex without protection, and contraception itself can fail: condoms break, the pill is forgotten, sometimes a man pretends to use a condom but removes it without consent in what is called "stealthing". Women are too often raped or forced into sex, especially in situations of conflict or migration, where there is no protection from pregnancy.

The way to reduce the numbers of abortions is by reducing sexual violence and coercion, and the best possible reproductive health services. The only way to save women from dangerous abortions is to make them legal and accessible. It is not pro-choice versus pro-life, pro-abortion versus anti-abortion. It is: stop the deaths of women (many of them already caring for children) because of attempts to stop legal and safe terminations, attempts which only increase the numbers of desperate and dangerous abortions, especially among the poorest women.

Abortion is a necessity when contraception fails. We can only hope to reduce the numbers, and prevent the deaths and the damage.

Wanted babies

The gap between rich and poor - countries and individuals - is not just about money. It is also about the decision-making gap, where the richer you are the more control you have of your own life and that of your children and other family members. This control means you are much less likely to get overwhelmed by those random life events that happen to all of us: illness, accidents, pregnancy, or having to care for family and friends when they need it. Without choices it is like being in rough seas that can destroy your fragile boat when there is nobody to rescue you if it overturns, or to tow you safely towards the harbour.

Family planning – for sexual and reproductive health - will not solve all the problems of poverty. Without it, though, those problems will only get worse. If family planning is combined with initiatives in the media, alongside better health services in poor areas and campaigns against child marriage, child sex and premature childbearing, other forced marriage, and female genital mutilation, the outcome for people now living in poverty can be transformative. The many successful projects in many parts of the world are now demonstrating just this.

Babies should be precious. They should be wanted and needed. Babies are our present and our key to the future. Let us have sex as we choose, without the worry of unwanted pregnancy. Let us all decide whether to have babies, and when is the right time for ourselves and for them, to give them the best possible childhood and the best future as adults. These are the biggest life decisions that anyone can make, and we should all be able to make these decisions for ourselves, for our communities and for our world.

Resources

Michelle Goldberg, *The Means of Reproduction: Sex, Power, and the Future of the World* (Penguin Press, New York, 2009).

I discuss the exclusion of women from development economics in my book, *The Domestication of Women: discrimination in developing societies* (Tavistock, Methuen and Kogan Page, 1980). Since then there have been many initiatives to incorporate women's work and lives into development programmes. However these have often managed to avoid the issue covered here, so crucial to women, of being able to decide when to have children.

Lynda Gilby & Meri Koivusalo (2020), "Universal health coverage: another political space in which to expand the elimination of sexual and reproductive health and reproductive rights," *Sexual and Reproductive Health Matters*, 28:2.

Chapter ten

TURNING THE DEBATE UPSIDE DOWN

If we are to make modern contraception and safe terminations available to all who need it, we are at a turning point. We have the methods, the tried and tested programmes, and the experienced personnel. What we now need is a serious and consistent commitment at all levels, from local to international.

If people's basic need to decide the number of their children is to be met, as an essential condition for economic development and safeguarding the planet, then we all need to break out of our comfort zone, tear up some of the rule books, and challenge many of the international bodies and individual governments. Here are a few suggestions.

Money talks

The whole **economic development** movement should stop ignoring women's and families' need to make their own life decisions. They should understand the critical importance for anti-poverty moves of improving women's and families' welfare, as well as the need to avoid the catastrophe of environmental damage and runaway climate change. This would be a very small part of the total spending required. According to one estimate, the cost of meeting existing levels of demand for family planning in the United States and all developing countries ranges from US$3.6 billion to US$4.6 billion per year, which is just 5% of the annual global spending on climate change adaptation and the mitigation measures agreed in the Paris Agreement on Climate Change.

Family planning projects should be eligible for **climate change adaptation funding**, and international organisations and governments should incorporate family planning into their development plans. Adaptation to climate change is an important Sustainable Development Goal in its own right (SDG13) alongside family planning, but the links are not being made.

More research is still needed on the **economic case** for family planning as an element in poverty reduction programmes. It has been estimated that a single dollar invested in family planning is worth six times that amount in other development approaches such as poverty reduction, education, or disaster preparedness. More data is required to reinforce this calculation, and the existing research needs to be better known. Deaths and injuries from unplanned pregnancies, and the negative effect on people's basic needs, should be valued as part of cost benefit analysis for development proposals. The real cost of supply failures, and illegal and dangerous abortion, should be fully understood in financial terms. Money talks, and this is especially true for economic development.

The IMF should help to focus policy-makers' attention on the failure of governments to take this seriously, by dropping its simplistic GDP calculation for national income (which can be artificially inflated by more people) and moving to **GDP per capita**. This would more accurately show the state of an economy in terms of its people's real income, and highlight the economic benefit of removing barriers to choice. US demographer Ron Lee argues that the "sweet spot" for this is 1.6 children per woman.

They should also attach an adequate value to the loss of a country's **natural resources** which result from population growth, including damage to soils, water and wild areas. As the environmentalist David Attenborough commented, speaking of human numbers in 2013:

> *"We have a finite environment - the planet. Anyone who thinks that you can have infinite growth in a finite environment is either a madman or an economist."*

The madmen (and women) have their own problems, but economists need to get on board now.

Microfinance organisations should recognise women's need for small loans to pay for healthcare, including contraception, safe abortion and maternity care, which so often requires the payment of fees as well as the cost of travel to the nearest clinic or hospital. The local boards deciding on small loans should set up a small panel of health visitors, nurses, midwives or doctors, with no affiliation to anti-choice groups, who would be able to decide on people's requests for healthcare loans while guaranteeing their confidentiality. These panels should have their own loan fund and be able to decide quickly about urgent cases. Not all individual health emergencies will be about pregnancy, but many will. The

Grameen Bank in India understands this but Europe-based Oiko Credit does not.

Those of us who give money to **international charities** should stop and think about what their policies are. Why would I give to Oxfam or Unicef, for example, when they refuse to help women when they most need it? I will give to one of the family planning service groups that target this need. I do not claim that this will solve all problems everywhere, as critics like to pretend we are saying. But directing our small contributions this way helps to fill the enormous imbalances which those "aid" organisations have created.

Health

Donor countries to the United Nations, its agencies and particular development funds and projects should give a greater proportion of their funding to **universal health care**, and insist that it must include family planning.

The govenments of low- and middle income countries should decide for themselves that health and family planning are a priority for their own policies and budgets. Much has been done in many of these countries by non-governmental organisations, backed by national and international aid agencies, to introduce high-quality health programmes. However they can never reach the numbers of people needing help unless governments put their own resources and **political priorities** into this. They could give much greater support and encouragement to the voluntary family planning organisations in their own countries. They should also encourage local government bodies, which often have their own budgets, to allocate serious funds to family planning.

Public money could be withheld from **religious-based hospitals** and clinics if they do not offer a full range of reproductive health services. In more than a dozen countries in Africa the "faith" sector - mainly Catholic - is estimated at over 30% of all health services. They often include high-cost private hospitals as well as district hospitals which oversee other health facilities, and they usually operate by formal agreements with the government concerned. In the Democratic Republic of Congo it is over 50%. In areas where only Catholic clinics and hospitals exist, a separate family planning service could be set up alongside a commitment that appropriate referrals would always be made. Alternatively, religious facilities can be incorporated into government health services, as has been done in South Africa. This should obviously be done carefully, preserving the best of these facilities while incorporating vital family planning services. There could be a crucial role for the WHO in advising on a transition process.

It is essential that universal health care should have a central role in all national and international **development plans**. The Covid-19 pandemic is proving how critical this is, and scientists are predicting a series of similar health crises in the years to come. Funding and planning for crises would protect the basic health services, including family planning, which need better and more secure funding protected from raids by emergency services.

All **development and aid programmes**, whether for major infrastructure, formal education, agricultural development or whatever, should incorporate basic health services where these do not already exist, and support existing services. This would provide an important confidence-building "quick win" element to the work, and also be of critical importance in its own right. The World Health Organisation (WHO) could draw up specifications for a minimum health service to underpin all programmes and projects.

WHO itself needs to include family planning in all its field work, and member States could pursue this at WHO meetings. At the moment **WHO** do excellent work in research and drawing up guidelines for family planning, but they need to go much further and demonstrate that they can integrate this fully into their practice.

All health programmes should include universal basic health care with reproductive health and choices as an integral element. It should become unthinkable to offer health support without this. **"Silo funding"** or so-called "vertical programmes" can mean a gleaming modern building for a particular disease and a shack with no facilities for maternity care next door. A particular issue arises with the public-private partnership, The Global Fund to Fight AIDS, Tuberculosis and Malaria, which raises and spends almost $4 billion a year. Anti-AIDS programmes have already diverted some of the funds that would otherwise have gone to family planning. It reinforces a perception that women's lives simply do not matter and that the world does not care about the people. Itt reinforces the alienation felt by some communities from modern medical care, including vaccination.

International health programmes, including the **"One Health"** movement (which started with a focus on zoonotic diseases passed from animals to humans) should widen their focus to include all human health issues including reproductive health. One Health is receiving very large amounts of funding from governments but currently seems to have little or no interest in human fertility. The funding should be conditional on their incorporating this crucial issue of health and welfare into all their work, otherwise it is not entitled to claim a One Health title.

From rights to needs

We should **switch the argument** in international forums from "rights" as in "SRHR" (sexual and reproductive health and rights) to "needs". The women's rights agenda, including freedom from sexual and other violence against women, will make better progress if it is not constantly challenged over "reproductive rights". Questions of child marriage, other forced marriage, rape and violence against women and FGM (female genital mutilation) should still be put forward as human rights issue. The same applies to LGBTI (lesbian, gay, bisexual, transsexual and intersex) rights. Human rights, and particularly women's rights, will move forward faster if separated from family planning. The reproductive health agenda will also work better if it is seen as a matter of basic needs and the fight against poverty.

The United Nations should consider abandoning its format for conferences on women's rights and reproductive health since these have so often been **sabotaged** by the Holy See, alone or with a small number of delegations, exploiting the requirement for unanimity.

Instead there should be consultations among all parties of good faith to draw up a **General Assembly** resolution on this. It would instruct all the specialised agencies - who are accountable to the General Assembly - to use their resources to support people's ability to make critical life decisions for themselves. There is a precedent for this in which I was involved: the General Assembly passed a resolution instructing the UN agencies to prepare practical measures for the support of the former Portuguese colonies. They all swung into action, producing stamps, draft regulations and other elements for independent governments to hit the ground running once the Portuguese withdrew. At one point I was impressed to meet an employee of the Universal Postal Union who had to rush off to her office to work on stamps as instructed by the General Assembly. Until then it had not seemed real.

This resolution can be passed by a simple majority in the General Assembly, unlike the special conferences where absolute consensus has been required (for no obvious reason) and can be vetoed by the Holy See and a few others. A majority in the General Assembly should be easily achievable. A resolution along these lines, enabling **all UN agencies** to support people's choices, could have a transformative effect for millions of people on the ground. The UN Fund for Population (UNFPA) could then become a source of **expertise and information** for all the agencies, and not just as the sole and insufficient source of operational funding.

Facing an unholy row

Permanent Representatives of member States at the UN should challenge the status of the **Holy See** delegation, and its lack of any legal basis, and demand that it should move to the same "observer" status as other world religions. There has been silence on this for far too long. Governments could also reconsider their "diplomatic relations" with the Holy See and move to a more realistic relationship which they would also apply to other world religions.

Researchers in the field of international law could usefully look into the status of the Holy See, to challenge its **unauthorised access** whether in the debates or behind the scenes, and recommend actions to stop its destructive tactics at the UN and at international conferences.

The current Pope, Francis, although he promised a "kinder and gentler" approach to human frailty rather than a condemnatory one, is not **changing the dogmas** on contraception and abortion. The hierarchy as a whole will - with differing degrees of severity - continue for a long time trying to instruct Catholics to follow the doctrine. However they must recognise that they should not abuse their access to national and international forums to impose their dogma on the vast majority of the world's people who are not Catholics or part of the Vatican's "crusade".

The Pope and the rest of the hierarchy should take a long, hard look at their **diplomatic machine** and its massive presence at international meetings, and cut it down to size. Persuasion is fine, coercion and manipulation are not. Their campaign against women's rights and especially family planning is damaging their reputation in the international community. They should also stop Catholic bishops' pressure on those governments with largely Catholic populations.

The Pope should also issue **guidelines** to those church members who wish to oppose abortion or contraception, forbidding them to use any form of abuse, violence or threats of violence whether against health personnel, patients or clinics.

He should pull back the funding for front organisations and websites which are putting out misinformation. The church's **huge expenditure** on international lobbying should be redirected to humanitarian assistance to all those in need, including the millions of women and children who are suffering from unsupported childbirth, malnutrition and ill-health, as well as from disasters, forced expulsions and war.

Those claiming to speak in the name of Islam and other **major religions**, especially in international forums, should also be challenged if they try use that to pursue an agenda which follows that of the Holy See. Religious leaders should listen to their own people, especially the women, if they really want to improve their welfare. They should certainly not try to impose their religious dogmas on members of other faiths, or no faith.

Priorities

There should be greater powers given to the initiative **"Every Woman Every Child"**, launched at UN headquarters by UN Secretary General Ban Ki-Moon in 2010, which aims to mobilise and intensify international and national action by governments, multilaterals, the private sector and non-governmental organisations. It needs greater resources, and be able to scrutinise work by the UN and its agencies to ensure that women and children are not left out.

The World Bank Group is unexpectedly becoming a leader in developing integrated health finance and delivery through its **Global Financing Facility** in Support of Every Woman, Every Child. The Bank should work with all the relevant UN agencies such as UNDP, WHO and Unicef so that they can match their programmes with the Bank's to improve universal health services to women and children.

The **habit of avoidance** of this issue by some international civil servants needs to be continually challenged. For example, the United Nations resolutions on Women, Peace and Security specify reproductive health as an essential component of the security and status of women. Yet the UN global indicators on Women, Peace and Security that monitor the implementation of these resolutions, issued in 2016, do not include reproductive health indicators or guidelines. Such inconsistencies are unacceptable for such a critical issue.

All those working in international agencies on the Sustainable Development Goals and international aid programmes should also be **required to include** reproductive health. At the moment its inclusion is random and inconsistent. Writing about two high-level meetings on the same day on 19 September 2016, the United Nations General Assembly's High-Level Meeting on Refugees and Migrants, and US President Obama's Leaders' Summit on Refugees, Alison Doody of 2020 Vision writes:

> *"The explicit inclusion of gender in high-level discussions is no longer remarkable, but remains inconsistent - sometimes taking priority, sometimes being mainstreamed into other issues, and at other times overlooked entirely. The situation is even starker, however, when it comes to sexual and reproductive health, which is too often still not given the priority of a life-saving intervention. This means SRH care can make it into one part of a declaration on refugees, but is entirely absent from another summit the same week."*

Another void is **food security.** Women and girls make up the majority of food-insecure people globally, and unwanted pregnancies add greatly to this burden. Yet it was omitted from the conversation on World Food Day of the same year.

Those who indulge in **censorship** of the issues should be challenged and, if necessary, disciplined. This is a matter for the Secretary General of the UN and the heads of all the UN agencies.

Leaving the comfort zone

Family planning organisations, whether national or international ones, should stop being defensive or even secretive, and **start communicating** widely about what they are doing. At the moment they are mainly preaching to the converted in terms of modern contraceptives and early abortion methods, and how these are best offered in different situations. I would hope to see open cross-sector consultations and conferences on a range of relevant topics, open to the whole development "Establishment": aid officials, women's and environmental groups, health organisations, and development practitioners and academics.

Show what you are doing, how and why. Tackle the ignorance of modern methods and the misinformation and prejudice that is being spread around by the opposition, such as imagined coercion or malpractice, and exaggerated claims about side effects from contraceptives.

A bit **less jargon** would also be welcome, with a real effort to speak the language of ordinary people and a clear-out of all the abbreviations and jargon. Needs: yes. Reproductive health: yes. Choices: yes. SRHR: no.

The **media** at all levels - local, national and international - should regularly report on health and family planning initiatives, and their successes. Too much "news" in this area is negative, focusing only on fundamentalist opposition, panics about "population decline" or ignoring these critical issues completely. There is a clear parallel with previous media coverage of climate change: too little, too conflicted, too late.

The whole international system should adopt the **mission statement** of the UNFPA:

> *"Delivering a world where every pregnancy is wanted, every childbirth is safe and every young person's potential is fulfilled."*

The people of the world, and future generations, depend on it.

A brief bibliography

I have done extensive searches of the literature on population growth and found no books that address this issue as one of women in development, or any that focus on the issue of individual decisions about children as key to overall population numbers. Almost all the authors are men and there is an avoidance of women's choices as key to this. The one exception is Michelle Goldberg's *The Means of Reproduction: Sex, power and the future of the world* (Penguin, New York, 2009) which examines the US and global battles over women's reproductive needs with reportage from areas of the conflict.

The most influential recent book in the UK is probably Danny Dorling's *Population 10 Billion* (Constable, 2013). However he fails to discuss in any detail the question of how people can prevent unwanted pregnancy, nor is there any acceptance of this being a women's issue. His references to contraception in general are dismissive. His conclusion - that "something" might appear which would solve the problem of human population growth - is complacent and in serious need of challenge.

There have been a number of alarmist books that warn of the dangers of rapidly increasing population, including Anne and Paul Ehrlich's *The Population Bomb* (Buccaneer, 1971 - note that Anne's name is omitted from some editions - and Stephen Emmott's *10 Billion* (Penguin, 2013). The titles show that they are looking at the numbers, not the individuals behind the numbers. Their failure to consider poverty or to discuss individual experience, or even family planning as an issue, leaves all their warnings at a level of abstract policy which is unlikely to be heeded. Books like these could even feed into the accusation that this is about "population control," a term which has proved damaging to efforts to promote people's real choices.

Lester R Brown has published a series of useful books about the environmental implications of population growth, including *Full Planet, Empty Plates* (Norton, 2012) and (with Hal Kane) *Full House* (Earthscan, 1995). Fred Pearce's *Peoplequake* (Eden Project, 2011) and Thomas L Friedman's *Hot, Flat, and Crowded* (Penguin, 2009) are similar, although the latter is welcome in describing the issue as one of women's needs. These and other such books are describing this as a key environmental issue, but they are very incomplete because they do not look at the solutions which lie among the people.

There is also the whole field of demography, which studies population changes including births, deaths and migration. They are generally working on statistical analysis rather than individual decisions. A useful academic contribution here is Sarah Harper's *How Population Change Will Transform our World* (Oxford University Press, 2016).

There is also a largely academic sub-genre of books debating the legacy of 19th century writers on population growth, particularly Thomas Malthus, who warned of mass starvation if populations increased, and Francis Galton, who coined the word "eugenics". I suggest that although these arguments seem to be endlessly fascinating to academics they should be consigned to history, since issues of the present day are more important and more urgent.

One of the sadder gaps in the literature is any move by influential campaigners like "The Elders" to include people's life choices into their human rights work. Mary Robinson, the former Irish President and now UN Special Envoy on Climate Change, is a case in point. Despite a proud record of helping to open up her own country to family planning she has almost nothing to say about these key issues as a factor in human welfare in poor countries, or their importance for biodiversity and the climate crisis, in her recent book *Climate Justice: Hope, resilience and the fight for a sustainable future* (Bloomsbury, 2018).

There is a specialist area of contraception and family planning studies (but not in book form) which offers a wealth of information, especially on the increasingly successful approaches to choice which are showing great success, in terms of improving contraceptive methods and also prog-rammes to make these available in areas where there are still major barriers to choice. This is very much preaching to the converted and there is an urgent need for more communication by family planning practitioners with specialists on health, economic development and the environment.

A critical element in this debate is what I am calling the New Eugenics - an alliance of religious fundamentalists, nationalists and sectarians, the Catholic Church hierarchy and various "pro-life" groups. There are several influential pro-natalist books: see Jonathan V Last's *What to Expect When No-one's Expecting* (Encounter Books, 2013), Mark Steyn's *America*

Alone: The End of the World as we Know it (Regnery Press, 2006), Pat Buchanan's *The Death of the West: How Dying Populations and Immigrant Invasions imperil our Country and Civilisation* (St Martin's Press, 2001) and several other titles which make it quite clear that they are promoting a pro-natalist agenda. Their ideas about needing to force population growth among Europeans and Americans are misogynist and often openly racist.

Books by Barbara Rogers

The Domestication of Women: discrimination in developing societies (Tavistock, Methuen and Kogan Page, 1980) is credited with boosting the integration of women into the international development process. Extensively reviewed, and a standard text on many development courses, it also led to invitations to speak at international conferences.

> "A cogent manifesto to which the scholarship of anthropology, economics, statistics, and development studies is convincingly harnessed." (*New Society*)

Men Only: An investigation into men's organisations (Pandora Press, 1988) tackled men's organisations and networks, and argued successfully for the abolition of public subsidies to men-only projects at private clubs in the UK, including Lords cricket ground.

> *"One always has a certain admiration for those who try to research primitive tribes, so I took my hat off this week to the doughty Ms Barbara Rogers… who set out to investigate the world of men's clubs."* (Sunday Times)

52%: getting women's power into politics (Women's Press, 1983) was the first book to look at a whole range of policy issues from women's point of view, and women's importance as swing voters. Extracts were published in *Woman* magazine entitled "So this is liberation".

> *"This is her vivid and controversial polemic, arguing that women must realise that traditional politics are too important to leave alone." (Time Out)*

Divide and Rule: South Africa's Bantustans (International Defence and Aid, various editions) described this key apartheid policy in detail. As the only publication on this subject, it contributed to the international refusal to recognise so-called "bantustans" as independent states.

Race: No peace without justice (World Council of Churches, 1980) is the result of extensive consultation among churches around the world, and has been used as an educational text since then.

The Nuclear Axis: The Secret Collaboration between West Germany and South Africa, with co-author Zdenek Cervenka (Times Books and Julian Friedmann Books, 1978) exposed *apartheid* South Africa's secret nuclear weapons programme. South Africa later became the first country in the world to acknowledge and dismantle its nuclear weapons.

***White Wealth and Black Poverty: American investments
in southern Africa*** (Greenwood Press, 1976) helped to kick-
start the movement to disinvest in *apartheid* South Africa.

> *"Rogers' forceful case for U.S. economic disengagement from
> South Africa is buttressed by a detailed description of the
> parallel development of apartheid and industrialization in
> South Africa... this study provides a valuable resource,
> superseding in breadth and depth most current analyses of the
> subject."*(Foreign Affairs)

About the author

Barbara Rogers has spent several years researching and writing about issues for women in lower-income countries. She has worked for the United Nations, WHO, the UN Development Programme and the Chair of the US House of Representatives Subcommittee on Africa, and followed up with research on economic development at the School of Development Studies, University of East Anglia. Her first book on the subject was *The Domestication of Women: Discrimination in developing societies.* This argued that development policies and programmes, by focusing on men, were seriously disturbing the balance in many traditional societies to impoverish women and make them more dependent – and that successful development had to involve the women on an equal basis. The book has contributed to a substantial shift in thinking about the role of women in development.

Barbara had a long break from writing after this to work for *Everywoman* magazine, Anti-Slavery International, Change and other non-governmental organisations. She later set up her own events business and an arts centre, but has always felt that there was much more to say on the subject of women's most important issue: being able to decide when to have children. She therefore returned to research on this, discovering that although the topic seemed simple and straightforward, in fact it is extremely controversial with entrenched "pro-life" positions coinciding with a taboo on discussion internationally. This means that the advances in contraception methods available, and in innovative projects and programmes, are little known outside the specialist family planning bodies – who themselves have retreated from public debate. This new book, *"Children by Choice?"* is intended to break through the stalemate and to reach out to women's and environmental organisations as well as health and economic development practitioners. Only by integrating choice programmes into all these areas, she argues, can the women and men living in poverty be given the choices they need.

Visit her website for news updates and comment on these issues: **www.childrenbychoice.net.**

.

Printed in Great Britain
by Amazon